T0270357

"If you want to be a healthy, bal[...] the keys."

—**RICK WARREN,** founding pastor, Saddleback Church

"Simple is not the same as easy. The Christian life is far from easy, but Max has taken something hard and made it much simpler for us. If you are looking for a place to jump-start your walk with God, get back to basics, or help someone start their journey with God on the right foot, *Don't Sink Your Own Ship* is a wonderful guide."

—**DR. MARCUS WARNER,** president, Deeper Walk International, author of *A Deeper Walk: A Proven Path for Developing a More Vibrant Faith*

"If I had read this when I was eighteen, it would have saved me a lot of heartache. This is a great guide, handbook, blueprint, road map, compass, trail, and foundation for life. Read it for yourself, and give it to your children."

—**STEPHEN ARTERBURN,** cofounder, Minirth-Meier New Life Clinics

"The wisdom of the Bible is designed to reveal the underlying moral and spiritual realities God has built into His creation. Max Anders has tapped into that wisdom to spell out for us some of the ways things work in God's world. Always readable and well-illustrated, *Don't Sink Your Own Ship* will help more than a few readers avoid some divinely placed brick walls and find the way God wills them to take."

—**DUANE LITFIN,** former president, Wheaton College

"Max Anders gives you a working knowledge of life's non-negotiables and a proven plan to turn them into 'second nature' traits in your heart."

—**TIM KIMMEL,** author, *Little House on the Freeway*

"Max has done it again! *Don't Sink Your Own Ship* is a must-read. It is simple, clear, biblical, entertaining, convicting, and life-changing. I teach a class on the spiritual life—I've just discovered an excellent text for that course. Max's insights, authenticity, and practicality make the book a ten-plus. I thoroughly and completely endorse it."

—**JOE C. ALDRICH**, former president, Multnomah Bible College and Seminary

DON'T SINK

YOUR OWN

SHIP

DON'T SINK
YOUR OWN
SHIP

20 SPIRITUAL LESSONS
YOU DON'T HAVE TO LEARN THE HARD WAY

MAX ANDERS

ZONDERVAN
REFLECTIVE

ZONDERVAN REFLECTIVE

Published in Grand Rapids, Michigan, by Zondervan. Zondervan is a registered trademark of The Zondervan Corporation, L.L.C., a wholly owned subsidiary of HarperCollins Christian Publishing, Inc.

Requests for information should be addressed to customercare@harpercollins.com.

Zondervan titles may be purchased in bulk for educational, business, fundraising, or sales promotional use. For information, please email SpecialMarkets@Zondervan.com.

ISBN 978-0-310-15623-9 (audio)

Library of Congress Cataloging-in-Publication Data

Names: Anders, Max E., 1947- author.
Title: Don't sink your own ship: 20 spiritual lessons you don't have to learn the hard way / Max Anders.
Description: Grand Rapids, Michigan: Zondervan Reflective, [2024]
Identifiers: LCCN 2023049634 (print) | LCCN 2023049635 (ebook) | ISBN 9780310156192 (softcover) | ISBN 9780310156215 (ebook)
Subjects: LCSH: Christian life--Miscellanea. | Spiritual formation--Miscellanea. | BISAC: RELIGION / Christian Living / Spiritual Growth | RELIGION / Christian Education / General Classification: LCC BV4501.3 .A5158 2024 (print) | LCC BV4501.3 (ebook) | DDC 248.4--dc23/eng/20240124
LC record available at https://lccn.loc.gov/2023049634
LC ebook record available at https://lccn.loc.gov/2023049635

Published in association with the literary agency of Wolgemuth & Associates, Inc.

Cover design: Tammy Johnson
Cover photo: © Biletskiy Evgeniy / iStock Getty Images Plus
Interior design: Kait Lamphere

Printed in the United States of America

24 25 26 27 28 LBC 5 4 3 2 1

This book is dedicated to our kids and their families who, short of Jesus, are the best thing that ever happened to us. Tanya, Philip, Natalya, Ivan, Chris, and Samantha

CONTENTS

INTRODUCTION

I want to make two points in this introduction.

First, this is not a deep book.

I didn't intend it to be.

Some of life's issues are deep and complex and require extensive investigation and deliberation.

Other issues can sometimes be fairly simple, relatively obvious, and occasionally easy to master if we just hear the wakeup call. Sometimes "a word to the wise" can be sufficient, and we can experience change fairly readily. That is the hope of this book.

However, the subjects in this book may uncover a need or desire within you to go deeper into a topic, in which case I've included discussion questions (for small groups or discipleship/mentoring relationships) or journaling questions (for personal introspection), as well as other books/resources.

But to begin, take a crack at the chapters. They may enable you to have some quick, easy wins in your Christian life. And if more needs to be done, you can go deeper, using this book as a helpful foundation and guide.

I've tried to make this book easy to read. It's generously punctuated with stories that are interesting, sometimes funny, and occasionally outrageous. But they all make a deceptively important point.

So, don't be your own worst enemy. Don't blow holes in the bottom of your own boat. Don't sink your own ship. Here are some vital spiritual truths you don't have to learn the hard way.

Second, this book is written for Christians. Everything in it presupposes that you are a Christian, that you believe the Bible, and that you are motivated to grow spiritually.

If you are not yet a Christian, that doesn't mean you cannot benefit from this book. But the ultimate benefit would be for you to become a Christian by reading it.

We live in a world that is becoming more and more resistant to the Christian faith. Yet, in spite of that, you may be drawn to Christianity in your life as the answer to the problems of the world as well as your own personal spiritual hunger.

I know that when I became a Christian, many years ago, I was going through a time of intense personal spiritual hunger, and I wanted to become a Christian regardless of the cultural pressures not to go down that path.

The Bible tells us that we cannot earn our salvation by being good or by anything we do for God. Rather, we are saved by believing in and receiving Christ and giving ourselves to Him.

When a man asks a woman to marry him, he is not looking for anything she can give him. He wants her! The same is true with God. He doesn't want anything we can give Him or do for Him. He wants us.

If you have not yet become a Christian, or are not sure, I urge you to make that decision now. Please visit www.peacewithgod .net. There you will find the information you need to guide you in your decision.

CHAPTER 1

LOOK TO GOD FOR HAPPINESS

Don't sink your own ship.
Look to God for happiness.

Happiness is not found by pursuing happiness. It is found by pursuing God.

In Your presence is fullness of joy;
In Your right hand there are pleasures forever.
—PSALM 16:11

I once heard of a man who was unhappy in his work, unhappy with his family, and unhappy with life in general, so he decided to escape to get away from it all. He joined a mute monastery, where he took a vow of silence. He could say only two words every five years. *This is perfect*, he thought. *No stress, no one to bug me, nothing but silence.*

So he stayed there five years without uttering a syllable. At the end of that time, his superior called the man into his office and said, "You have two words you can speak. Would you like to say anything?"

The guy nodded his head and said, "Bad food!"

1

He went for another five years without uttering a syllable, and again his superior called him into his office and asked if he would like to say anything.

He nodded his head and said, "Hard bed!"

Another five years passed, and the man's superior called him in and asked him if he would like to say anything.

The guy said, "I quit!"

His superior responded, "Well, I'm not surprised. You've done nothing but complain since you got here!"

Our friend thought that joining a mute monastery would make him happy. But it didn't. The reason is that happiness is not based on external circumstances. It's based on internal attitude.

Think of all the wealthy people you know of who are miserable, and then think of all the people of modest means who are happy. This simple observation tells us that there is no direct correlation between external circumstances and happiness. Abraham Lincoln once said, "A man is about as happy as he makes up his mind to be."

1. What most people say they want out of life is to be happy.

What most people say they want out of life is to be h_____.

Most Americans say that their highest aim in life is to be happy. It is perhaps the highest value in American culture. That value goes back as far as our Declaration of Independence:

> We hold these truths to be self-evident, that all men are created equal, that they are endowed by their Creator with certain unalienable rights, that among these are life, liberty, and the pursuit of happiness.

This theme of happiness pops up time and time again in American culture. When pondering choices to be made, relationships to pursue, or dreams to chase, the guiding phrase is typically: "I just want to be happy." When we give counsel to others on the same issues, it is: "I just want *you* to be happy."

There is certainly nothing wrong in wanting to be happy. In fact, the pursuit of happiness seems to be woven into the fabric of the human psyche. All people have different ideas as to what it would take to make them happy, but everyone pursues happiness. Some pursue it in wealth, others pursue it in achievements, and others pursue it in pleasure, but all pursue happiness.

Blaise Pascal, a seventeenth-century philosopher, once wrote:

> All men seek happiness. This is without exception. Whatever different means they employ, they all tend to this end. The cause of some going to war, and of others avoiding it, is the same desire in both, attended with different views. The will never takes the least step but to this object. This is the motive of every action of every man, even of those who hang themselves.[1]

2. God created us to long for happiness, and He uses that longing to draw us to Himself.

God created us to long for happiness, and He uses that longing to d_____ us to Himself.

As Christians, we may be vaguely uncomfortable admitting that happiness is a priority for us. This doesn't sound spiritual. Yet the Bible doesn't seem to shy away from presenting happiness as a valid longing:

> As the deer pants for the water brooks,
> So my soul pants for You, God.
> My soul thirsts for God, for the living God.
> (Psalm 42:1–2)

God, You are my God; I shall be watching for You;
My soul thirsts for You, my flesh yearns for You,
In a dry and exhausted land where there is no water.
    (Psalm 63:1)

You will make known to me the way of life;
In Your presence is fullness of joy;
In Your right hand there are pleasures forever.
    (Psalm 16:11)

In these verses, the Bible speaks of deep longings we have and implies that the fulfillment of these longings, as well as joy and pleasure, are things God does not find objectionable. Rather, He seems to encourage these, as long as our pursuit of happiness is centered in Him.

3. We cannot control circumstances completely enough for them to keep us happy.

We cannot c_____ circumstances completely enough for them to keep us happy.

If happiness for us comes only through maintaining a sufficient flow of favorable circumstances, life will be pretty hard on most of us. First, we cannot be happy merely with pleasurable circumstances. Pleasurable circumstances make good frosting but not a good cake. Second, even if circumstances *could* make us happy, we cannot control them adequately enough to bring us consistent happiness.

A prime example of this is found in Charles Kuralt's book *A Life on the Road*. Many years ago, Kuralt was host of both *Sunday Morning*, a weekly television program, and *On the Road* specials on CBS in which he traveled around the United States in a motor home and filmed interesting stories about unusual people or happenings.

Portions of his work often aired on *The CBS Evening News with Walter Cronkite*. Every evening when Cronkite, one of the most respected men in America at the time, completed his newscast, he signed off in his distinctive voice and style, "And that's the way it is." This was one of the most famous phrases in America for decades.

Kuralt wrote:

A woman wrote me a letter from Ohio. She said her parakeet could say, "And that's the way it is," like Walter Cronkite. We went there right away, of course. As soon as she opened the door, the parakeet said, "And that's the way it is!" While we set up the lights and camera there in the living room, the parakeet watched us from inside his cage and said, "And that's the way it is!" We pointed the lens at the cage and started rolling. The parakeet looked at the camera and said:

"Aaaawk!"

The parakeet's owner said, "And that's the way it is!" to give him a cue.

The parakeet said, "Aaaawk!"

"And that's the way it is!" she said patiently.

He said, "Aaaawk!"

We turned off the lights to let the parakeet calm down. We went into the kitchen and had a cup of coffee and talked about the weather and other things. Then we sauntered back into the living room, pretending to pay no attention to the parakeet in his cage. The bird's owner thought this might work. We said nothing. The parakeet said nothing. We turned on the camera again.

The parakeet said, "Aaaawk!"

After an hour or two of this, we packed up, promising to return some other time. We said good-bye to the disappointed woman who wanted to see her parakeet on Walter Cronkite's news program. We closed the front door and started down the

walk to the driveway, carrying our camera and lights. Behind us
in the living room, we heard the parakeet say:

"And that's the way it is!"[2]

And that *is* the way it is. You try to control circumstances, and
you can't.

Solomon told us this three thousand years ago, but we don't
quite believe him. Solomon, king of Israel, was likely handsome
enough to be a male model. He was brilliant. He was incompre-
hensibly wealthy. He was commander in chief of a powerful army
and king of a great nation.

With all this going for him, Solomon admitted that he did
not withhold anything from himself. If he wanted it, he got it.
He lived a rich, full life in the terms of this world. But as an old
man, he said that all the things this world had to offer were unsat-
isfying: "Everything is meaningless . . . completely meaningless"
(Ecclesiastes 12:8 NLT). In the end he wrote, "Fear God and obey
his commands, for this is everyone's duty. God will judge us for
everything we do, including every secret thing, whether good or
bad" (Ecclesiastes 12:13–14 NLT).

Our problem is that we don't quite believe Solomon. We think
that for some unknown reason he just didn't get it right. Yes, he had
brains, money, looks, fame, and power—and still wasn't happy—
but if *we* had his brains, money, looks, fame, and power, *we* would
be happy. We would be able to pull it off.

Yet, by contrast in her book *Life, Liberty and the Pursuit of
Happiness*, Peggy Noonan wrote insightfully:

> It is a terrible thing when people lose God. Life is difficult and
> people are afraid, and to be without God is to lose man's great
> source of consolation and coherence.
>
> I think we have lost the old knowledge that happiness is
> overrated—that, in a way, life is overrated. We have lost somehow

a sense of mystery—about us, our purpose, our meaning, our role. Our ancestors believed in two worlds, and understood this to be the solitary, poor, nasty, brutish and short one. We are the first generations of man that actually expected to find happiness here on earth, and our search for it has caused such unhappiness. The reason: if you do not believe in another, higher world, if you believe only in the flat material world around you, if you believe that this is your only chance at happiness—if that is what you believe, then you are more than disappointed when the world does not give you a good measure of its riches, you are in despair.[3]

So true! If we pursue happiness in what this temporal world alone has to offer us, then life can be a profound disappointment. However, pursue God and the fullness of the life He offers, and happiness dawns like the sun after a dark night.

4. We can increase our happiness by focusing on gratitude.

We can increase our happiness by focusing on g_____.

It is easy to get preoccupied with the wants and desires we have that God has *not* met and lose sight of the things He *has* given us. This is like a child who is ungrateful to his parents because he did not get the Christmas presents he wanted, rather than being grateful for food, clothing, shelter, education, medical attention, life opportunity, and familial love that he *has* been given.

A key to entering into the love-relationship God offers us is to *cultivate gratitude* for what He *has* given us, rather than being ungrateful for what He *hasn't*. Gratitude is a fundamental virtue. If we cultivate gratitude, many other virtues click into place.

Here is a short list of things God has given to His children that we often *take for granted*. Don't read over this section lightly. It is easy to think, "Yeah, yeah . . . blah, blah, blah . . . that's what you're supposed to say."

Rather, internalize these truths. They are powerful and transforming if we grasp them, if we take them in, if we comprehend them, and if we understand what life would be like without them. Try to imagine any one of these truths not being true or being taken away, or which one you might willingly give up.

1. **God offers us His love.**
   Scripture: "See how great a love the Father has given us, that we would be called children of God; and *in fact* we are." —*1 John 3:1*

   Quote: "We are born for love. It is the principle of existence and its only end." —*Benjamin Disraeli*

2. **God offers us His forgiveness.**
   Scripture: "As far as the east is from the west, so far has He removed our wrongdoings from us." —*Psalm 103:12*

   Quote: "To be a Christian means to forgive the inexcusable, because God has forgiven the inexcusable in you." —*C. S. Lewis*

3. **We are born again, spiritually.**
   Scripture: "You have been born again not of seed which is perishable, but imperishable." —*1 Peter 1:23*

   Quote: "For all have sinned and fall short of the glory of God—whether they stand at the heights of political power or the depths of prison confinement. I have been in both spots. And no matter where a person is, God will meet him or her there with an invitation to forgiveness and new life." —*Chuck Colson*

4. We will live forever in paradise.

Scripture: "He will wipe away every tear from [our] eyes; and there will no longer be *any* death; there will no longer be *any* mourning, or crying, or pain . . ."

—*Revelation 21:4*

Quote: "Has this world been so kind to you that you should leave with regret? There are better things ahead than any we leave behind."   —*C. S. Lewis*

5. We are given the dignity of causality.

Scripture: "For we are His workmanship, created in Christ Jesus for good works, which God prepared beforehand so that we would walk in them."   —*Ephesians 2:10*

Quote: "'God,' said Pascal, 'instituted prayer in order to lend to His creatures the dignity of causality.' But not only prayer; whenever we act at all He lends us that dignity. It is not really stranger, nor less strange, that my prayers should affect the course of events than that my other actions should do so.

For He seems to do nothing of Himself which He can possibly delegate to His creatures. He commands us to do slowly and blunderingly what He could do perfectly and in the twinkling of an eye. This is how (no light matter) God makes something—indeed, makes gods—out of nothing."   —*C. S. Lewis*

6. We receive disproportionate eternal reward for things suffered in this life.

Scripture: "For I consider that the sufferings of this present time are not worthy to be compared with the glory that is to be revealed to us."   —*Romans 8:18*

Quote: "On the day of the Lord—the day that God makes everything right, the day that everything sad becomes untrue—on that day the same thing will happen to your own hurts and sadness. You will find that the worst things that ever happened to you will in the end only enhance your eternal delight. On that day, all of it will be turned inside out and you will know joy beyond the walls of the world. The joy of your glory will be that much greater for every scar you bear."   —*Timothy Keller*

7. We will share in God's glory.

Scripture: "For our momentary, light affliction is producing for us an eternal weight of glory far beyond all comparison."   —*2 Corinthians 4:17*

Quote: "It is a serious thing to live in a society of possible gods and goddesses, to remember that the dullest most uninteresting person you can talk to may one day be a creature which, if you saw it now, you would be strongly tempted to worship . . . There are no ordinary people. You have never talked to a mere mortal."

—*C. S. Lewis*

Just imagine that God were to give you that *something* you might most want from Him right now (career, relationship, health, financial freedom), but, in return, take away any one of the seven things I just mentioned. What a calamity! What a broken decision! What a hopelessly bad trade. Internalizing this truth helps put into perspective the majesty of God's benevolent intentions toward us.

Of course, we all go through times in life when we are knocked off balance by a major disruptive experience . . . the death of a loved one, the loss of a job, or a serious injury or illness. Times of crisis are more challenging than times of non-crisis. But, in typical everyday life, once we have laid a foundation for overall happiness by putting God at the center of our lives, we gain daily happiness largely by cultivating gratitude and taking pleasure out of the little things in life rather than demanding a succession of big things.

If you added up all the times you were happy from the big things, you would be lucky to be happy for a year out of your whole life. But if you allow yourself to be happy over little things, happiness becomes a much more frequent visitor. Let me mention a few of the things that make me happy:

- my wife's smile
- the chickadees at my bird feeder
- the delicate lemon-yellow daylilies that bloom in July
- a blue sky on a clear day
- the different colors of green in the new growth of spring
- two babies looking at each other in amazement at the grocery store checkout line
- the smell of dinner cooking
- the sound of a child's laughter
- a photograph of good friends
- a recording of music I like
- returning the wave of someone I see while I'm driving
- the taste of fresh fruit in season
- an unexpected phone call from a friend
- the chiming of the pendulum clock in my study
- watching friends and family meeting at the airport
- the stained-glass windows in a fancy church
- a golden retriever puppy
- a postcard from a friend on vacation
- moonlight shimmering on the lake
- the sight of a horse grazing in a field
- the architecture of the courthouse in my hometown
- a nearby field of wildflowers

Some time back, I began to develop the habit of imagining what life would be like without the various things I enjoy. Imagine if there were no food, clothing, and shelter. Imagine if you did not have anyone to love you or anyone to love. Imagine what life would be like without valuable things to do. Imagine what life would be like if you didn't have those things to brighten your life. Not good!

This practice helped me in three ways:

1. It made me more *aware* of the things I liked.
2. It made me more *appreciative* of the things I have and enjoy.
3. It increased my *capacity* for happiness.

I am so deeply grateful that I can see, hear, smell, touch, and taste. I am so grateful I can read. I am so grateful for my wife, my family, and my friends. I am so grateful I live in a country where the Bible is readily available and I can worship as I please. I am so grateful I don't have to worry about where my next meal is coming from. I am so grateful for electricity so I can read at night, run the air conditioning, and turn on the faucet for a drink. I am so grateful I have people I love and people who love me.

Perhaps another way of saying this is that *joy* in life depends on accepting the will of God in our lives and focusing on His love and what He has done for us, is doing for us, and will do for us. And then there's the Great Joy Rainbow over all of life: *in the end, all will be well.*

In contrast, *happiness* in life for a Christian is built on joy, but is then greatly enriched by cultivating gratitude . . . the ability to notice and appreciate the ordinary things in life, realizing that if you didn't have them, they wouldn't seem so ordinary. When we're in a crisis, it's hard to glean happiness from these ordinary things. Our world shrinks until it is just us and the crisis. But when the crisis passes, happiness in life depends on appreciating the little things (which, in reality, are not necessarily little). The big things don't come along often enough to keep us happy. But there is no end to the little things.

The *surest* road to happiness is living for God, placing our ultimate hope in the next world, and learning to be grateful for the small things that come our way in this world.

So, don't sink your own ship.
Look to God for happiness.

CHAPTER REVIEW

Repetition is the key to mental ownership.

Happiness is not found by pursuing happiness. It is found by pursuing God.

1. What most people say they want out of life is to be
   h_____.
2. God created us to long for happiness, and He uses that
   longing to d_____ us to Himself.
3. We cannot c_____ circumstances completely
   enough for them to keep us happy.
4. We can increase our happiness by focusing on
   g_____.

 DON'T SINK YOUR OWN SHIP

If something is important, you must repeat it until it changes you.

Chapter Summary
1. Look to God for h_____.

 LIFE-CHECK

Answer these questions, either individually by journaling the answer or in a spiritual accountability group.

1. What do you think of the statement "The chief end of mankind is to glorify God by enjoying Him forever"? Does it ring true to you?
2. How would you evaluate Peggy Noonan's statement that happiness is overrated and we need to refocus on the "higher world" as the ultimate source of happiness?
3. Can you list the little, ordinary things in life that give you happiness? How do you think you could expand your list?

FOR FURTHER REFLECTION

Additional Scripture. (Some Bibles use "blessed" instead of "happy.")

Psalm 16:11	Proverbs 17:1
Psalm 42:2	John 13:17
Psalm 63:1–2	Galatians 5:22–23
Proverbs 16:20	

 RESOURCES

For further study.

30 Days to Growing in Your Faith (Chapter 1), Max Anders

Happiness, Randy Alcorn

CHAPTER 2

REPENT QUICKLY WHEN YOU SIN

Don't sink your own ship.
Repent quickly when you sin.

The key to living a holy life is "ready repentance" of sin.

Like the Holy One who called you, be holy yourselves also in all your behavior, because it is written: "You shall be holy, for I am holy."

—1 PETER 1:15-16

I was in big trouble. It was Friday afternoon, and I desperately needed a haircut before I flew out to teach an all-day seminar the next day. I didn't have enough time to go to my regular barber, so I called a large establishment near my home, the one where the sign said they cut both men's and women's hair. They said they could get me in right away.

I jumped in the car and took off. As I was driving, a sense of foreboding came rolling over me like fog off a swamp. The memory of bad haircuts at the hands of new barbers flashed back vividly. But what was I to do? I was in a bind.

I parked the car and walked toward the front door. I don't

remember the name of the place, but for reasons that will become clear, I refer to it now as *Delilah's Den*.

As soon as I walked in, I knew that my darkest fears would be realized. The air was thick with perfume. Heavy, sensual music throbbed so loudly through speakers that I could feel it vibrating in my chest. *Boom-babba boom-babba boom-babba!!!*

I am often insecure when I feel out of place. This was years ago, and I was dressed very conservatively by comparison to everyone else in that place. Hair, clothes, demeanor—they all looked as though they had stepped off the pages of a fashion magazine. I was momentarily stunned.

I looked like a penguin in a flock of flamingos.

Feeling uneasy about looking so "different," I decided I had to get out of there. I turned on my heels to leave and nearly flattened a receptionist who had snuck up behind me.

"Do you have an appointment?" she asked with eager anticipation.

"Uh, yes," I admitted, my ears radiating my embarrassment. "My name is Max Anders."

"Oh, yes, Mr. Anders. I've scheduled you with Delilah (not her real name—I don't remember her real name). She's just finishing up with someone and will be ready for you in just a moment. Why don't you go over to Cleopatra (not her real name, either). She'll shampoo your hair and get you ready for Delilah."

The shop was one big, open room, with a couple dozen hair-washing and cutting booths around the perimeter that opened to the middle. I walked across that center area to Cleopatra's booth. Dozens of pairs of eyes burned into the back of my head while I stared at my shoes.

Cleopatra put me in a tilt-back chair that deposited my head in a sink behind me and began washing my hair. I can't explain how she did it, but she seemed to be sudsing my head in an unusually friendly manner. Then she rinsed, sudsed again, rinsed, conditioned, and rinsed. Delilah still wasn't ready for me, so Cleopatra began to massage my head. She asked me if it felt good. It felt wonderful, but I hated to admit it.

We made small talk. I probably seemed relaxed on the outside, but inside I was screaming, *"Let me out of here!"* My toes curled under in my shoes. My fingernails dug into my kneecaps. My jaw muscles tensed convulsively. *What am I doing here? What if someone in my church sees me here with Cleopatra, acting like we are long-lost friends?* I could see the headlines in the paper: *"Local Pastor Gets Haircut at Delilah's Den!"* Subheading: *"Under Pressure, Admits to Enjoying Scalp Massage!"*

Finally, Delilah was ready for me. I got out of Cleopatra's chair and again slunk across the room, my eyes darting nervously. I crawled reluctantly into Delilah's chair, and in response to her questions I shouted how I wanted my hair cut. (We both had to talk very loudly to be heard over the deafening *Boom-babba, boom-babba*.) As Delilah began to cut, the music stopped abruptly, just in time to allow her to shout into the tomblike silence, "And what do you do, Mr. Anders?"

Every head in the place seemed to turn in my direction. The suddenness of the music stopping, the volume of Delilah's ill-timed question, and the clear cultural difference between me and every other person in the place gave them all an intense interest in my answer. They all strained to hear.

I cracked.

I felt so out of place, so conspicuous, and so insecure about being so different that I did the only thing that occurred to me at that moment.

I lied!

"I'm a landscape architect," I heard myself croak.

That answer seemed to satisfy everyone. Their heads turned back, the music started up again, and their world returned to normal. But mine collapsed. *Landscape architect? Why did I say that?*

I don't know a thing about landscaping. Why didn't I tell her I was a pastor?!? Because I'm a chicken. I'm an overeducated, undercommitted, gutless wonder! I admitted to myself.

Haircut finished and back in my office, I slumped in my chair like someone who had just lost everything. I was overwhelmed with remorse. I laid my head on my desk and absorbed the crushing weight of my shame and guilt.

As the Holy Spirit drove back and forth over me like a steamroller over a hunk of human asphalt, I realized that the profound conviction under which I was buried was not a result of having told a "white lie." Rather, it was because, out of insecurity and fear, I had publicly denied Jesus.

I had lied to save my own emotional skin, just as Peter had lied the night Jesus was betrayed. I now knew I would have done exactly what he did. I would have hidden in the shadows while Jesus was taken to the cross.

As I sat there, my head on my desk, my hands sprawled out in front of me, breathing laboriously into my desk pad, the thought slowly dawned on me what I had to do. I had confessed my sin to God. Now I had to call Delilah, confess my sin to her, and ask her to forgive me.

It was the last thing in the world I wanted to do, but I envisioned Delilah randomly visiting our church the next Sunday and wondering what in the world a landscape architect was doing in the pulpit (when I told her this story, an elder's wife remarked compassionately, "I hope you didn't tell her what church you pastored!"). In addition, the Holy Spirit had me face down on the sidewalk and wasn't letting me up.

When Delilah came to the phone, I said, "When you asked me what I did for a living, I felt out of place and embarrassed, and I didn't tell you the truth. I told you I was a landscape architect. But I'm not. I'm the pastor of a local church. It was wrong for me to lie to you, and I would like to ask if you would forgive me."

Delilah didn't know what to say. She began to babble. "Oh, don't worry about that, Mr. Anders. Lots of people have second jobs . . . Why, I didn't think a thing . . . Heavens, it doesn't . . . Don't give it a second thought."

"You don't understand," I returned. "I don't have a second job. I made it up because I felt insecure and embarrassed to tell you that I was a pastor. That was wrong of me, and it would mean a great deal if I could know you forgive me."

This went on for a while, with me asking forgiveness and Delilah talking a blue streak around it. Finally, one last time, I acknowledged my sin and asked if she would forgive me. When she at last realized I was not going to let her go until she said she forgave me, she said she forgave me. I thanked her and hung up the phone. The steamroller drove off of me, and I began to come back to life.

I am so grateful to the Lord for the power of His conviction and for His refusal to let me go until I had done the right thing. I am so glad He held me to the standard of His holiness.

1. We Christians can live a life of holiness by repenting quickly when we sin.

We Christians can live a life of holiness by r_____ q_____ when we sin.

Holiness is not a matter of becoming a monk or a saint. Nor is holiness a matter of never sinning.

If that were the case, holiness would be an unreachable goal for all of us. Rather, holiness is a matter of ready repentance. When the Holy Spirit, whose ministry is to convict us of our sins, *does* convict us, and we readily repent, then we are capable of living a life of practical holiness.

My experience at Delilah's Den happened many years ago, and in retrospect I think God used that situation in a very significant way to strengthen and protect me. I fear my life could have become a continuous struggle every time I got in a situation where I felt intimidated, with subsequent follow-up lies following me like a swarm of mosquitoes after a sweaty fisherman. In fact, I think this could have led to bigger and bigger lies and, perhaps, even eventual moral failure. I know this may sound extreme, but *I've never known of anyone who fell into big sin who hadn't gotten there by first tolerating little sins.*

The mandate for holiness is found in 1 Peter 1:15–16: "Like the Holy One who called you, be holy yourselves also in all your behavior, because it is written, 'You shall be holy, for I am holy.'"

The holiness referred to here doesn't mean our perfect holiness in heaven. It means practical holiness *now!* Peter says, "be holy . . . *in all your behavior!*" (emphasis added). Because God knows that we cannot become sinlessly perfect while still on this earth (Romans 7:14–25), He has provided a way for us to live lives of practical holiness by cultivating a spirit of ready repentance.

2. Repentance makes us usable by God.

Repentance makes us u_____ by God.

Walk with me through Isaiah 6:1–8, and we will see the practical result of repentance:

In the year of King Uzziah's death I saw the Lord sitting on a throne, lofty and exalted, with the train of His robe filling the temple. Seraphim were standing above Him, each having six wings: with two each covered his face, and with two each covered his feet, and with two each flew. And one called out to another and said:

"Holy, Holy, Holy, is the LORD of armies.
The whole earth is full of His glory."

And the foundations of the thresholds trembled at the voice
of him who called out, while the temple was filling with smoke.
(vv. 1–4)

In this passage we see that God is absolutely holy. He is so
totally superior to us that we can only respond one way to His
presence: acknowledgment of our sin and ready repentance.

Then I said:

> "Woe to me, for I am ruined!
> Because I am a man of unclean lips,
> And I live among a people of unclean lips;
> For my eyes have seen the King, the LORD of armies."
> (v. 5)

When Isaiah saw God's holiness, he felt a deep sense of his own
sin, and he repented deeply.

> Then one of the seraphim flew to me with a burning coal in
> his hand, which he had taken from the altar with tongs. He
> touched my mouth with it and said, "Behold, this has touched
> your lips; and your guilt is taken away and atonement is made
> for your sin." (vv. 6–7)

When Isaiah repented deeply, God forgave completely.

> Then I heard the voice of the Lord, saying, "Whom shall I send,
> and who will go for Us?" Then I said, "Here am I. Send me!"
> (v. 8)

When Isaiah was forgiven, God offered to use him, and Isaiah
accepted.

3. We can cultivate a greater spirit of ready repentance by expanding our understanding of God's relentless grace.

We can cultivate a greater spirit of ready repentance by expanding our understanding of God's r_____ grace.

Here are five observations on holiness adapted from *Rediscovering Holiness*, by James I. Packer:

1. *To repent means, literally, to turn around.*

    Once you were walking north, and now you turn around and walk south. When God reveals a sinful attitude or value, it means we abandon it and adopt its opposite.[1]

2. *God's agenda for the rest of our lives on earth is our growth into greater lifestyle holiness.*

    The God into whose hands we have placed ourselves is in the holiness business. Part of the answer to the recurring question we so often ask—"Why is this happening to me?"—is that God is using a painful experience to build into us Christlike virtue.[2]

3. *The great task of holiness is to grow up by growing down.*

    Christians become greater by getting smaller. Pride blows us up like balloons, but grace punctures our conceit and lets the hot, proud air out of our system. We bow to events that rub our noses in the reality of our own weaknesses, and we look to God for strength to cope.[3]

4. *As we grow spiritually, we become more aware of sin.*

    We learn we will never stop falling short of God's character. As a result, those who are going forward into greater holiness may have the impression, from time to time, that they are going backward. They are not.[4]

5. *When we sin, it doesn't mean our salvation is jeopardized.*

It just means our fellowship with God is broken. Just as when we sin against our spouse, it doesn't dissolve our marriage, but it dissolves our fellowship. With the relationship intact, we restore fellowship by repentance and forgiveness.[5]

Other chapters in *Rediscovering Holiness* deal with specific differences that will be made in our life as we progress into holiness. For now, I want to reiterate the main point for this chapter: holiness this side of heaven does not mean never sinning. Rather, it means repenting readily when we do sin. As the apostle Paul wrote, "I . . . do my best to maintain a blameless conscience both before God and before other people, always" (Acts 24:16).

In conclusion, whenever our conscience condemns us, we repent, ask forgiveness from God and others (if necessary), and provide restitution (if necessary). Then our conscience is cleared. We are now blameless and usable by God. If we initiate this process as soon as the Holy Spirit convicts us of sin, we are living a life of practical holiness.

SO, DON'T SINK YOUR OWN SHIP.
REPENT QUICKLY WHEN YOU SIN.

CHAPTER REVIEW

Repetition is the key to mental ownership.

The key to living a holy life is "ready repentance" of sin.

1. We Christians can live a life of holiness by r_____ q_____ when we sin.
2. Repentance makes us u_____ by God.
3. We can cultivate a greater spirit of ready repentance by expanding our understanding of God's r_____ grace.

 DON'T SINK YOUR OWN SHIP

If something is important, you must repeat it until it changes you.

Chapter Summaries

1. Look to God for h_____.
2. R_____ q_____ when you sin.

 LIFE-CHECK

Complete these exercises, either individually by journaling the answers or in a spiritual accountability group.

1. Read Isaiah 6:1–8 and 1 Peter 1:15–16. Then ask the Holy Spirit to reveal to you anything in your life you need to repent of. Make a list. Then, one item at a time, go through the list and repent. (Don't wait until you *feel* forgiven to accept God's forgiveness. Remember that repentance is an act of the will, not a function of the emotions.) If any restitution or asking of forgiveness needs to be done, plan how to do this. Ask God to give you a clear conscience as a result of going through this process. If you feel you need help, find someone who

is spiritually mature, whose spiritual life you admire, and ask this person to assist you (pastor, Bible teacher, counselor, mentor, friend, etc.).

2. What causes you the most difficulty in your pursuit of holiness? Anger? Fear? Depression? Materialism? Sensuality? Covetousness? What do you think you could do to ensure you are making satisfactory progress in that area? List all the possibilities. Then prioritize them and begin to work on at least the first one.

3. What experience(s) have you had that interfere with your pursuit of holiness? This is sometimes related to one of your weaknesses. At other times it is related to the values you learned growing up or some difficult experiences you had as a child. Is there something else beyond what you did in number 2 that you might be able to do to increase your victory over that experience?

 FOR FURTHER REFLECTION

Additional Scripture.

Isaiah 6:1–8

Acts 24:16

Ephesians 4:24

Hebrews 12:5–11 (note verse 10)

1 Peter 1:15–16

 RESOURCES

For further study.

30 Days to Growing in Your Faith (Chapter 16), Max Anders

Rediscovering Holiness, James Packer

CHAPTER 3

BE TOTALLY OBEDIENT TO GOD

Don't sink your own ship.
Be totally obedient to God.

The shortest distance between you and the life you long for is total obedience to Christ.

If you keep My commandments, you will remain in My love; just as I have kept My Father's commandments and remain in His love. These things I have spoken to you so that My joy may be in you, and that your joy may be made full.
—JOHN 15:10-11

When I was in graduate school, I worked at a clinic that provided remedial therapy for children with mild learning disabilities. It was a rewarding experience, as I saw many obviously bright children struggling with poor grades and frequent discipline problems in school turn into good students.

As part of the therapy, we gave the students assignments to do and then went into an adjoining room where we could watch them through a two-way mirror. The students were told that we would be behind the mirror watching them, but some

29

often had very short attention spans and soon forgot that we were there. They would goof off, disrupt others, and forget about their assignments.

When the students drifted from their assignment, we reentered the room to help them, reminded them that we were watching, and got them refocused on their responsibility. We used this technique to help the children develop longer attention spans.

It was often comical to see the children begin to lose concentration. Often, they would look up from their work slightly glassy eyed and begin to glance aimlessly around the room. Then they might look right at the mirror, wrinkle their noses or stick out their tongues, or straighten their hair. They frequently pestered their neighbors. It amazed me that they so easily lost sight of the fact that we were behind the mirror looking at them.

Our reentering the room always snapped the children back to reality. With red faces and embarrassed grins, they resumed their work. Over time, as they finally "got it" that we were behind the mirror, most of the students were able to lengthen their concentration span considerably, which helped them to do better in school.

Doesn't this remind you of our relationship with God? Life is lived in front of a spiritual two-way mirror. God can see us, but we can't see Him. There are things we know we should or should not do, but God is not "in the room." We can't see Him, and over time we lose sight of Him. We even begin to think that He isn't there anymore. So, we stick out our tongues at heaven or walk around goofing off or disrupting our neighbors.

Life would go so much better for us if we would only remember that God is behind the mirror. We have spiritual learning disabilities. We have short spiritual attention spans. We're supposed to be manifesting the character and proclaiming the name of Jesus, but instead we often find ourselves goofing off or acting badly.

1. When we disobey God, He allows us to suffer the consequences of sin.

When we disobey God, He allows us to suffer the c_____ of sin.

When this difficult situation happens, God "comes into the room" to help us, to do something to enable us to grow, mature, and deepen.

We cannot break the laws of God. We can only break ourselves against His laws when we ignore or violate them. We think we can ignore the truth and get away with it. We can't. We think we can sidestep obedience to God whenever we want without paying a price. We can't.

There is always a price, and the price is in proportion to the sin. Some sins have a greater consequence than others. The sin of mild laziness does not have as great a consequence as sexual promiscuity, for example. But there is always a price.

2. There are cause-effect consequences of sin, and/or divine-discipline consequences of sin.

There are c_____-e_____ consequences of sin, and/or d_____-d_____ consequences of sin.

The price of disobedience comes in two forms. First, it comes in the natural cause-and-effect consequences of our actions. If we are mildly lazy, for example, we might miss out on a promotion at work that would have paid us more money. No thunderbolt comes down out of the sky to strike us dead. But we paid a price anyway—a natural, cause-and-effect price.

On a more sober note, if we are sexually promiscuous, we may pay a greater price: sexually transmitted diseases; depression, anxiety, or other emotional problems; or an unwanted pregnancy. No thunderbolt comes out of heaven to zap us. It's just that people who are sexually promiscuous often pay a high price—this is part of the natural scheme of things. Galatians 6:7–8 says, "Do not be deceived, God is not mocked; for whatever a man sows, that he will also reap. For he who sows to his flesh will of the flesh reap corruption."

On the other hand, God does at times bring direct judgment into the life of a person for sins committed. A thunderbolt, as it were, sometimes zaps us from heaven. We read in Hebrews 12:5–6: "My son, do not regard lightly the discipline of the LORD, nor faint when you are punished by Him; for whom the LORD loves He disciplines, and He punishes every son whom He accepts."

The link between our sin and the consequence may or may not be apparent. But we have the word of Scripture on it that our sin may very well result in direct divine discipline.

From this we see that there is always a price to be paid for disobedience. Sometimes it is the natural consequence of our actions. Other times it is divine discipline. But there is always a price.

3. God requires obedience from us because He loves us and everything He asks of us is to give something good to us or keep some harm from us.

God requires obedience from us because He loves us and everything He asks of us is to give something g_____ to us or keep some h_____ from us.

Like an athlete under a closely scrutinized training program, a musician in a carefully monitored practicing regimen, or a soldier involved in preparation for special warfare, there is no wasted motion with God. Every action, every attitude, and every rehearsal contributes to the ultimate goal. If we get lazy or careless or rebellious, it only delays the realization of His ultimate goal for us.

We read in Psalm 19:7–11:

> The Law of the LORD is perfect, restoring the soul;
> The testimony of the LORD is sure, making wise the
> simple.
> The precepts of the LORD are right, rejoicing the heart;
> The commandment of the LORD is pure, enlightening
> the eyes.
> The fear of the LORD is clean, enduring forever;
> The judgments of the LORD are true; they are righteous
> altogether.
> They are more desirable than gold, yes, than much
> pure gold;
> Sweeter also than honey and drippings of the honeycomb.
> Moreover, Your servant is warned by them;
> In keeping them there is great reward.

If these words are true—and of course they are—it would be idiotic to willfully disobey the Lord. Yet, in spite of everything, we are disobedient! We forget God is behind the mirror. This is self-defeating. This is self-destructive. This is counterproductive. This keeps us from enjoying the very things we want from life. But we disobey anyway.

On the other side of the ledger, we find the opposite conclusion: A person is blessed by God when he is obedient to Him. In John 15:10–11 we read,

> If you keep My commandments, you will remain in My love; just as I have kept My Father's commandments and remain in His love. These things I have spoken to you so that My joy may be in you, and that your joy may be made full.

So we see in this passage that joy is a consequence of obedience. Great blessings come to the person who is scrupulously obedient from the heart to the Scriptures.

If we believe obedience is the shortest distance between us and the life we want, we will obey. If we disobey, it is because our faith has broken down. We don't believe obedience will bring happiness. Or we believe a little disobedience will hurt only a little bit. Obedience is not nearly as hard if we become persuaded that it's not only for God's glory but also for our good.

We said earlier that we cannot break the laws of God. We can only break ourselves against them when we violate them. When we mature to the point that we "get" this truth, it can give us the resolve to do what is right.

When we come to the point at which we really believe that true happiness lies in following God and not self, we can gain the power to turn from sin.

Some years ago, my wife and I went to a professional dog show and, in observing the relationship between *man and dog*, received instruction on the relationship between *God and man* and on *the rewards of obedience*.

The show took place on a large, square green of closely mowed grass where the dogs were put through a number of obedience trials, which included:

1. One at a time, the dogs had to start, stop, change directions, sit, stay, and return to their masters, following a prescribed course that took them all over the lawn, without any verbal commands . . . only hand signals.
2. Out of a pile of wooden dumbbells, which were each identical to one another except for their identification numbers, each dog had to select the one wooden dumbbell which its master had handled.
3. On command, the dogs had to jump back and forth over a high, solid wooden hurdle. Again, only hand signs were used.
4. The dogs were required to sit in the center of the lawn.

Upon being told to "stay," each dog was required to remain there for three minutes while its trainer was out of sight in a tent.

Two dogs in particular stood out. One was a large white German shepherd. He was an eager, grinning, tongue-lolling, fun-loving dog, but not fully trained. While enduring the "sit-stay" command, he spied a rabbit hopping leisurely around the back edge of the lawn. The large, well-muscled paragon of canine virtue began trembling like a white Jell-O statue, eyes riveted in utter absorption on this rodent treasure.

As though deliberately baiting the dog, the rabbit began cavorting playfully around the base of a mesquite bush, gamboling about in utter ecstasy under the inflamed scrutiny of the shepherd.

One final tantalizing hop was more than the white powder keg could endure, and, as though shot out of a cannon, the shepherd exploded in the direction of the rabbit.

Both disappeared quickly into the bush, not to be seen in public again. While it was entertaining to watch, the dog's "display of obedience" was a failure and an embarrassment to its owner. Untrained, it did not yet attain to that marvel of harmony and communication that exists between skillful trainer and well-trained dog.

In contrast to the white German shepherd was a glorious, silky golden retriever. The retriever's excellence was as great as the shepherd's failure. Obedience to every command was instantaneous and perfect. Before, during, and after each command, the eyes of the golden were, rather than roaming the horizon for signs of life, fixed devotedly . . . no, adoringly . . . on the young girl who was its owner and trainer. After each drill, the dog would return to her side and, with its head up, stare into her eyes for the next command.

After all the dogs had gone through the trials, the trainers and canines lined up for the awards. Fourth prize went to a springer spaniel, third to a German shepherd, second to a black Lab.

All during this time, the golden retriever sat obediently beside its master, looking up into her eyes.

Finally, first prize went to this marvelous dog and the girl who trained it. A polite ripple of applause washed through the audience. Then the crowd and contestants began to disperse.

As they did, a marvelous thing happened.

The girl wheeled to face her dog, squealed with delight, and began clapping her hands together excitedly. At this, the dog lunged up toward the girl's face in a desperate attempt to lick her in the mouth. She laughed and pushed him back. He tried again. She began running toward her car, laughing, clapping in unbridled joy as her dog barked and jumped and circled around her all the way, sharing completely in her joy.

Chills played up and down my spine as I openly admired the joy, the intimacy, the trust, the devotion, and the adoration that flowed between dog and girl.

The intelligence, athletic ability, courage, and personality latent within this dog was developed to a higher degree, and displayed more effectively, than any other dog I had ever seen. I thought, *this is the highest good to which I have ever seen canine life elevated*. This was a marvel—a tribute to itself and its master.

But everyone knew that the skill, intelligence, insight, patience, and personality of the owner were also on display. A lesser trainer could not have gotten so much from her charge. Glory to the dog! Glory to the owner!

Had that dog been left to its own world, it would have been just a dog, an ignorant slave of its basic instincts to eat, run, and bark.

There were likely times in the training process when the dog was unhappy. It likely wanted to quit and run away. The owner may have often wondered if the dog would ever learn. But after the training process, the dog was happier and more fulfilled at its master's side than anywhere else in the world. The dog received that which it most wanted out of life from its relationship with its master.

So, in the Great Obedience Trial of life, are we golden retrievers or are we white German shepherds? Are we out in the hinterlands chasing the rabbits of this world, or are we fellowshipping with our Master in the joy of obedience? The decision is ours—to obey and enjoy God, or to disobey and bring on ourselves the cause/effect consequences of sin, as well as the discipline of our loving heavenly Father.

- In John 15:10–11 we read, "If you keep My commandments, you will remain in My love; just as I have kept My Father's commandments and remain in His love. These things I have spoken to you so that My joy may be in you, and <u>that your joy may be made full</u>."
- In Psalm 1:1–3 we read, "Blessed is the person who does not walk in the counsel of the wicked . . . but his delight is in the Law of the LORD, and on His law he meditates day and night. He will be like a tree planted by streams of water, which yields its fruit in its season, and its leaf does not wither; and in <u>whatever he does, he prospers</u>."

If we believe that obedience is the shortest distance between us and the life we want, we obey. But if we disobey, it is because we don't believe obedience will bring us the greatest happiness. Obedience is not nearly as hard when we become persuaded that it is not only for God's glory, but also for our good.

SO, DON'T SINK YOUR OWN SHIP.
BE TOTALLY OBEDIENT TO GOD.

CHAPTER REVIEW

Repetition is the key to mental ownership.

The shortest distance between you and the life you long for is total obedience to Christ.

1. When we disobey God, He allows us to suffer the
   c_____ of sin.
2. There are c_____-e_____ consequences of sin, and/or
   d_____-d_____ consequences of sin.
3. God requires obedience from us because He loves us and everything He asks of us is to give something g_____ to us or keep some h_____ from us.

 DON'T SINK YOUR OWN SHIP

If something is important, you must repeat it until it changes you.

Chapter Summaries
1. Look to God for h_____.
2. R_____ q_____ when you sin.
3. Be totally o_____ to God.

 LIFE-CHECK

Answer these questions, either individually by journaling the answer or in a spiritual accountability group.

1. Does it ever seem to you as though life is a two-way mirror: that God can see you, but you can't see God? Do you ever do things you know you shouldn't do because it seems like God isn't around? How do you think you can keep a clearer picture of the presence of God in your life?

38

2. Can you remember a time when you "broke" yourself against a law of God? That is, did you violate a commandment of God's and then pay a bad price for it? What insights does that experience give you for similar situations in the future?

3. Would you say you are more like the golden retriever or the German shepherd? What are some of the "cottontails" of this world that tempt you to flee in disobedience from the presence of God?

 FOR FURTHER REFLECTION

Additional Scripture.

John 15:10–11	Galatians 6:7–8
Acts 5:27–29	2 Thessalonians 1:6–8
Romans 6:17–18	1 Peter 1:22

 RESOURCES

For further study.

30 Days to Growing in Your Faith (Chapters 12, 18), Max Anders

What You Need to Know about Spiritual Growth (Chapter 9), Max Anders

CHAPTER 4

BE A GOOD STEWARD OF LIFE'S RESOURCES

DON'T SINK YOUR OWN SHIP.
BE A GOOD STEWARD OF LIFE'S RESOURCES.

Stewards own nothing, but manage the possessions and affairs of another.

It is required of stewards that one be found trustworthy.
—1 CORINTHIANS 4:2

Some years ago when I was teaching at a Christian college, an older student told of a time when he was working in a chicken processing plant in Alaska. The chickens were terminated, dipped in scalding water, and placed on a conveyor belt. The belt fed the chickens into a box-shaped gizmo at the end that had a million rubber fingers whirling madly on the top, bottom, left, and right, with only a small hole in the middle for the chickens to pass through. They came out the other side without a feather on them, ready for additional processing.

One of the coworkers at the time was relentlessly obnoxious and spent a great deal of time harassing other workers and his boss. It was not merely irritating, but truly insufferable. The boss was a very quiet man who rarely spoke, but one day he was the brunt of an unrelenting verbal assault which eventually took him past his limit. He picked the offender up and threw him onto the conveyor belt, which immediately fed the man through the whirling gizmo. According to the eyewitness, he popped out the other side beet-red, with not a stitch of clothes on!

For many of us, that is a parable of life. Sometimes things build up and make us feel as though someone has picked us up and thrown us on the conveyor belt of life, feeding us through a whirling gizmo (which includes our work, the house, the car, the family, the lawn, the neighbors, the daily news, our finances, our health, etc.). We end up on the other side, beet-red, with nothing left to give.

So, what do we do when life tries to take more from us than we can give?

To begin with, we must understand and accept that we are stewards, not owners, of life's resources and we are to invest them to fulfill God's will, not our own. That way, God determines our consequences in life, not us. He does not ask us to be successful; He only asks us to be faithful.

A steward is someone who administers the possessions and affairs of another. Properly seen, we have nothing of our own. Everything we have belongs to God, and is to be managed according to God's priorities (Matthew 25:14–30).

Everyone has been given the same set of resources: time, talent, and treasures. We don't all have the same measure or degree, but we all have some of each. So, we are each to use our time as the Lord wants us to, our talent as the Lord wants us to, and our treasure as the Lord wants us to. That is the essence of being a steward.

Jesus taught in the parable of the talents in Matthew 25:14–30 that we are all responsible to use wisely what God has entrusted to us. The apostle Paul wrote in 1 Corinthians 6:19–20: "Or do you not know that your body is a temple of the Holy Spirit within you, whom you have from God, and that you are not your own? For you have been bought for a price; therefore glorify God in your body."

Nothing we have, not even our bodies, is our own. Everything we have belongs to God, and we are to use it in a way that glorifies Him.

1. We steward our time by balancing faithfulness to God's priorities with not committing to more than we can do.

*We steward our time by balancing faithfulness to God's p_____
with not committing to m____ than we can do.*

We all have bad "time" days. I heard a story about a man whose secretary buzzed him one day and asked who was in his office with him. He said, "Oh, no one. It's just me. I'm beside myself." Shortly after that, he got in his car to go home and drove off in all directions! It was a bad day!

The pressures can get so great, and our world moves so fast, that managing our time according to our priorities can be a significant challenge. Yet we each have an equal amount of time: twenty-four hours a day. In the Scriptures, we read concerning time:

- Be careful how you walk, not as unwise people but as wise, making the most of your time, because the days are evil (Ephesians 5:15–16).
- Conduct yourselves with wisdom toward outsiders, making the most of the opportunity (Colossians 4:5).
- Teach us to number our days, that we may present to You a heart of wisdom (Psalm 90:12).

This is not a time management book, so we cannot go into detail on time management principles. But I just want to make the point that it matters to God how we use our time. Our affairs are

His affairs. Our time is His time, and we are to steward our time according to His priorities.

Likely, we fall into one of two camps:

1. We are careless about our use of time, and need to be more disciplined to use our time according to God's priorities and not our own.
2. We are diligent about our use of time, and need to guard against getting overwhelmed with our inability to get as much done as we would like.

No matter which camp we are in, we can fall back on key biblical principles. God expects us to be responsible and do our best, but He does not expect us to do better than we are able.

Several tag lines have been helpful for me:

- All we can do is all we can do; and then we can't do any more.
- There is always time to do the will of God.
- We are called, not to be successful, but to be faithful.

So, use your time wisely but do not embrace the burden of trying to do more than you are able.

Finding God's balance is the key to stewarding our time.

2. We steward our talent by using our gifts to fulfill our God-given calling.

We steward our talent by using our gifts to fulfill our God-given c_____.

Our elderly friend Wilma used to say, "There are lots of things I can't do, but I can bake a pie."

Bake pies she did, and she would take them to those who moved into the neighborhood. Then, as she chatted with her new friends and got to know them, she would steer the conversation to the Lord and would tell them about Jesus.

She didn't have a *lot* of talent, but she used well what she was given.

Before we were even born, God planned good works that He wanted us to do. Ephesians 2:10 says, "For we are His workmanship, created in Christ Jesus for good works, which God prepared beforehand so that we would walk in them." Amazing!

We're all a part of the spiritual body of Christ, and each of us matters. There are no insignificant people in the family of God. We are created to serve God. We have each been given gifts and abilities to use to serve Him, His people, and His Kingdom. First Peter 4:10 says, "As each one has received a special gift, employ it in serving one another as good stewards of the multifaceted grace of God."

If understanding your spiritual gift is new to you, I have listed a website at the end of this chapter that will explain spiritual gifts and offer you an inventory to suggest what your spiritual gift(s) might be. One question that I have found helpful over the years is to ask, "If you could do anything you wanted to do for God and knew that you would succeed, what would you do?" This thing may not be exactly what God wants you to do, but I have found that asking such a question does a pretty good job of heading you in the right direction.

You might also end up doing something that is a variation of your first choice, but it can likewise help start you thinking in the right direction.

We are managers of the gifts God has given to us. They may be great or small in our eyes, but they all matter to God. As 1 Corinthians 4:2 says, "It is required of stewards that one be found trustworthy." *God has made an investment in us, and He desires a return on that investment.*

It doesn't matter what our talent is. It may be an artistic talent, an academic talent, a physical talent, an organizational talent, a practical talent, or a spiritual gift. Whatever it is, we must ask the Lord how He wants us to use it for His glory.

Toward the end of His life Jesus prayed, "I glorified You on the earth by accomplishing the work which You have given Me to do" (John 17:4). We can take rich joy and satisfaction in using our talents, whatever they are, to accomplish the work God has given us to do. This glorifies God.

3. We steward our treasure by showing God that He has our heart—by how we use our money.

We steward our treasure by showing God that He has our h_____—by how we use our m_____.

Mark Twain was attending a meeting where a missionary had been invited to speak. Twain was deeply impressed. Later, he was reported to have said:

> The preacher's voice was beautiful. He told us about the sufferings of the natives, and he pleaded for help with such moving simplicity that I mentally doubled the fifty cents I had intended to put in the plate. He described the pitiful misery of those savages so vividly that the dollar I had in mind gradually rose to five. Then that preacher continued, and I felt that all the cash I had carried on me would be insufficient, and I decided to write a large check. Then he went on and I abandoned the idea of the check. And he went on, and I got back to five dollars. And he went on, and I got back to four, two, one. And still he went on. And when the plate came around, I took ten cents out of it.

That is *not* the perspective we are to have on our money. We are to view it as God's, and to be willing to give of our finances to help advance the spread of the gospel, regardless of how long a preacher preaches.

Luke 12:33–34 teaches that we are to lay up treasures in heaven, not on earth, because *where our treasure is, there will our hearts be.*

One of the things God asks us to do is to give back to him a portion of what He has given us. Why would He make this request? The answer is that He does not need our money, but He wants our hearts. A primary way God tests our hearts is to ask us for money.

Haggai 2:8 tells us, "The silver is Mine and the gold is Mine." Deuteronomy 8:18 says, "Remember the LORD your God, for it is He who is giving you power to make wealth."

Obviously, we need money to put food in our stomachs, clothes on our backs, and a roof over our heads. There are many other things that normal life requires us to spend money on. God doesn't expect us to give all our money away. But we are to give as generously as we can, while still maintaining our God-given responsibilities (2 Corinthians 8–9). Pray and ask God for guidance on what you should give. Giving not only is required to serve the Lord, but giving *generously* keeps our heads clear and our hearts warm.

Each person has five primary areas of responsibility: personal, family, church, work, and society.

Here are some examples of these responsibilities:

1. *Personal:* spiritual life, health, talents, intellectual growth, personal growth, finances, hobbies
2. *Family:* parents, siblings, spouse, children, extended family
3. *Church:* spiritual gifts, evangelism, financial support, fellowship
4. *Work:* personal responsibilities, boss, coworkers, clients, general public, vocational growth
5. *Society:* voting, being a good citizen, being a good neighbor, helping the disadvantaged

We are to direct our time, talents, and treasures into these areas of responsibility according to scriptural principles and the leading of God. How this occurs will be different for each person, and this can be tricky. Sometimes we feel like the ship that was carrying a cargo of yo-yos and got caught in a terrible storm off the coast of California. It sank seven times! When we try to keep everything afloat, we may sink seven times. But we keep working at it, praying about it, and getting better at being good stewards in the areas of our responsibility.

So, don't sink your own ship.
Be a good steward of life's resources.

CHAPTER REVIEW

Repetition is the key to mental ownership.

Stewards own nothing, but manage the possessions and affairs of another.

1. We steward our time by balancing faithfulness to God's p_____ with not committing to m_____ than we can do.
2. We steward our talent by using our gifts to fulfill our God-given c_____.
3. We steward our treasure by showing God that He has our h_____—by how we use our m_____.

 DON'T SINK YOUR OWN SHIP

If something is important, you must repeat it until it changes you.

Chapter Summaries
1. Look to God for h_____.
2. R_____ q_____ when you sin.
3. Be totally o_____ to God.
4. Be a good s_____ of life's resources.

 LIFE-CHECK

Answer these questions, either individually by journaling the answer or in a spiritual accountability group.

1. Do you know what your life priorities are? Do you use your time according to your life priorities? If you don't, set aside the time necessary to establish your priorities and begin to use your time accordingly. (Stephen Covey's book *The 7 Habits of Highly Effective People* is an excellent resource for doing this.)

2. What are your strongest talents, gifts, or abilities? Are you using them according to the Lord's priorities? Is there anything you ought to begin doing or stop doing in order to use your abilities properly? If you would like additional help discerning your spiritual gift(s), visit the website listed in the resources section.

3. Do you have your finances under control? Do you support a local church and other worthy causes with your money? Do you think you are using your money the way the Lord would? What changes do you think you might need to make? If necessary, are you willing to make them? (Randy Alcorn's book *The Treasure Principle* is an excellent resource for working through this.)

 FOR FURTHER REFLECTION

Additional Scripture.

Psalm 39:5	1 Corinthians 4:1–2
Psalm 90:12	1 Corinthians 6:19–20
Matthew 25:14–30	2 Corinthians 8:13–14
Luke 16:1–13	Galatians 6:10
Romans 11:35–36	Ephesians 5:15–16
Romans 14:7–8	Colossians 4:5

 RESOURCES

For further study.

Time: *The 7 Habits of Highly Effective People*, Stephen Covey

Talent: *What You Need to Know about the Holy Spirit* (Chapter 6), Max Anders

Spiritual gifts inventory: https://gifts.churchgrowth.org/spiritual-gifts-survey/

Treasure: *The Treasure Principle*, Randy Alcorn

CHAPTER 5

BE A SERVANT TO OTHERS

Don't sink your own ship.
Be a servant to others.

We are created by God to serve others.

For even the Son of Man did not come to be served, but to
serve, and to give His life as a ransom for many.
—MARK 10:45

We have all heard of "barn raisings" which were common in rural America in the eighteenth and nineteenth centuries. Men would gather at a building site where there were precut beams and lumber. Under the direction of experienced builders, the men would put up a post-and-beam frame on a foundation that was already laid. The roof and siding went on quickly thereafter, with entire barns often being completed in a single day. During the process, wives cooked enough food to feed the crew as children gawked at the proceedings or went off to play.

In such communities in rural America, this was a very real kind of social security. The residents knew that if they helped build a barn for their neighbors when they needed it, their neighbors would build a barn for them if they should ever need it. It was a band of people who all agreed to look out for the welfare of the others, knowing that the others would look out for them.

A hundred or two hundred years of cultural upheaval later, many Americans hardly know how to live in fellowship and harmony with others. The characteristics which foster fellowship and harmony are often seen as weakness or stupidity: serving others, admitting when we are wrong and apologizing, giving the benefit of a doubt, going the extra mile, turning the other cheek, giving time and money to others when you may not ever have the favor returned, etc. Or, even worse, serving others can open us to being taken advantage of. As a result, we now often live as a collection of little human islands, in proximity to others but not in communion. It makes for lonely people and a harder life.

1. The Bible teaches that Christians especially are to have a servant's heart and serve one another.

The Bible teaches that Christians especially are to have a s_____ heart and serve one another.

The Bible teaches that Christians are to live as servants to one another. We read in Mark 10 that two of Jesus's disciples, James and John, asked to be given positions of honor when Jesus established His kingdom. The other ten disciples got pushed out of shape about it, and so Jesus called them together to solve the dispute:

> You know that those who are recognized as rulers of the Gentiles domineer over them; and their people in high position exercise authority over them. But it is not this way among you; rather, whoever wants to become prominent among you shall be your servant; and whoever wants to be first among you shall be slave of all. For even the Son of Man did not come to be served, but to serve, and to give His life as a ransom for many. (Mark 10:42–45)

Not only did Jesus teach this, but He lived it. He washed His own followers' grimy feet, a chore normally reserved for a slave (John 13). This was a revolutionary message in a culture which was very "class conscious." He did so for the specific purpose of teaching the disciples that they should serve one another. Power, position, and privilege were keenly sought after everywhere, among both Jews and Romans. Jesus was definitely swimming upstream.

Later, the apostles also taught the principles of servanthood. Paul wrote, in Philippians 2:1–4, one of the most eloquent statements ever made about the heart of a servant:

> Therefore if there is any encouragement in Christ, if any consolation of love, if any fellowship of the Spirit, if any affection and compassion, make my joy complete by being of the same mind, maintaining the same love, united in spirit, intent on one purpose. Do nothing from selfishness or empty conceit, but with humility consider one another as more important than yourselves; do not *merely* look out for your own personal interests, but also for the interests of others.

What's more, even those in authority are to serve those under them. All authority is to be used benevolently for the good of those under authority, whether it is husband/wife relationships (Ephesians 5:22–31), parent/child relationships (Ephesians 6:1–4), employer/employee relationships (Ephesians 6:5–9), government/citizen relationships (1 Peter 2:13–14), or church/member relationships (1 Peter 5:1–4).

In all cases, those in power are to use their position for the good and welfare of those under authority. That is the spirit of servant leadership.

Chuck Colson, in his book *A Dangerous Grace*, wrote:

> Nothing distinguishes the kingdoms of man from the kingdom of God more than their diametrically opposed views of the

exercise of power. One seeks to control people, the other to serve people; one promotes self, the other prostrates self; one seeks prestige and position, the other lifts up the lowly and despised. As citizens of the Kingdom today practice this view of power, they are setting an example for their neighbors by modeling servanthood.

Does it cost anything to live this way? Of course! But what we get in return is a spirit of unity and harmony, along with the added benefit of others' looking out for us when we are in need. The way God has ordained things, we get not by taking, but by giving.

2. We can serve by doing *what we can* to meet the needs of others.

We can serve by doing what we can *to meet the n_____ of others.*

We cannot help everyone. So, we can demonstrate servanthood today by *giving what we can* to help meet the needs of others. Even Jesus admitted that the poor would always be with us. Even Jesus ate while others were hungry. If we gave away all our money, we would not make a dent in poverty, and our own families would starve. If we spent 100% of our time serving others, we would soon dry up. Even Jesus rested. Nevertheless, we *are* to help others in need *when it lies within our power to do so*.

In the parable of the good Samaritan, we learn five principles for deciding when to help others:

1. When people come across our path (we don't have to go looking for them)
2. They have a true need (not just a desire) that they cannot meet by themselves
3. Meeting the need would not enable dysfunction (don't reward self-destructive behavior)

4. We have the resources to meet the need (time, talent, *and* treasure)

5. Then, God may want us to meet the need

If someone meets these criteria, we may meet their needs. If not, we don't. So, in this context, how do we serve others? There are many ways. The following stories are all true, although names and some details of circumstances have been changed to protect anonymity (* = not their real names).

Serving John

Susan* and John* were married under pretty ordinary circumstances and began living a pretty ordinary life. Their relationship was neither a blessing nor a curse; it was somewhere in the middle. As time passed, they both began to change, but in opposite ways. Susan began to feel a stirring, a hunger in her heart for something more than this world was offering. John, on the other hand, began to "dull out." He worked too hard, watched too much television, and drank too much beer. He lost interest in most everything around him, including Susan.

The pain of the boredom and rejection in the marriage finally got to Susan, and she began to "let herself go." An attractive woman, she no longer kept herself looking attractive, began to nag and criticize John, quit cooking meals, and began spending a lot of time with other ladies who had similar marriages.

However, in the course of events, Susan became a Christian. While her fundamental desires changed, she still stumbled a little in her approach. Now, instead of nagging John about not mowing the lawn or about watching too much television, Susan nagged him about going to church with her. Things got worse instead of better.

When Susan learned the Scriptures better and understood that her role was to respect her husband even if she did not respect his lifestyle, she made an important decision. Instead of trying to change John, she decided to change herself. Susan chose to just love him as best as she could, and give her life to Jesus as completely as a missionary or a nun would. She gave up her expectations to get what she wanted out of this life, dedicated herself to serving Jesus, and put her hope in the next life.

Susan quit nagging John, started taking better care of herself, quit running around, began cooking again, and took on an air of peace about herself that was new to John.

Obviously, John noticed. He tested her severely. He reacted negatively to nearly everything she had done. He questioned her motives about why she was looking better, criticized her new healthy cooking, and mercilessly ridiculed her about going to church.

However, since Susan had not made these changes in order to change John, but to serve Jesus, she stuck to her guns. Finally, the weight of the change broke John. At first, he simply quit attacking her. Then he began to be nice to her. Finally, John himself became a Christian, and while much of the change in his life came more slowly than Susan's, he did change, and their marriage became an example of spiritual unity.

Susan's attitude of servanthood was very costly and painful for her. She had no guarantees that John would change, nor is it an indication that if another woman acts the way Susan did that her husband will change. But Susan's desire was to serve Jesus by serving her husband. How her husband responded was not the determining issue in her faithfulness. Rather, it was the affirmation of God.

That is one way of being a servant in today's world.

Serving Billy

Billy* was a six-year-old terror. He made Dennis the Menace look like a choir boy. His primary goal in life appeared to be to make his neighbor Jim's life miserable. For instance, Jim* drove home one day to find his prized apple tree stripped of fruit, which was scattered all over the ground. Another day, the same fate befell his peaches. Yet another day, Billy repeatedly ran his three-wheeler trike into Jim's garage door, leaving black marks on the white paint. Still another time, Billy turned on the water sprinkling system while Jim was working in the yard, soaking him.

Jim's response to all these infractions was always the same. First, he glared at Billy and growled viscous threats. Then he went to Billy's mother and lodged his complaints through gritted teeth. Billy's mother forced an insincere apology from Billy and the curtain was closed on that event, only to open on another soon after.

One day after being away on vacation, Jim and his wife pulled back into their driveway only to see Billy sitting on the top bar of the chain-link fence, looking as though he had spent the entire time plotting his next disaster. For some reason, Jim saw Billy in a new light. When he got out of the car, Jim said, "Hi, Billy. Did you have a nice Christmas?"

Billy looked stunned.

"What did you get for Christmas?"

Cautiously, Billy began to describe his gifts, warming up quickly in the process. Then, in a tone of voice Jim had never heard before, he said, "What did you get for Christmas, Mr. Johnson?"

Billy's stare wasn't blank anymore. His eyes had come alive. There was interest there . . . an appeal for friendship. He smiled. Jim smiled. The war was over. They chatted for a while, and Jim showed Billy some tools he got for Christmas. In the months that followed, a friendship blossomed. Billy was no longer Jim's tormentor; he became a curious, generous, lovable next-door neighbor.

That's yet another way we can serve others.

Serving the Homeless

He couldn't believe it. Fred* had often driven past the homeless shelter on his way to work and wondered how those people ended up that way. Then, through a series of unfortunate coincidences,

Fred found himself out of a job. On top of that, his family's home burned as a result of faulty wiring. All their possessions were destroyed, and because Fred did not have a job, they could not get another home. Suddenly, he was "one of them." Homeless.

Fred and his family moved into the homeless shelter, but he was consumed with bitterness and humiliation. He was a stick of human dynamite with a short fuse. He finally got another job, but it would be months before they could save enough money to get back into a house. Fred eventually realized that his attitude was affecting the happiness of his wife, his children, and everyone around him. He prayed for God's help to cope with his circumstances.

The shame began to melt away, and Fred decided that while he was in the shelter, he would try to help others deal with the humiliation and shame they were feeling. One day, he spoke to an elderly gentleman with an angry countenance. The conversation broke the ice, and the gentleman grew less angry over the following weeks.

In the remaining months Fred talked to as many people as he could, and if they let him, he prayed with them. The cold freeze which seemed to inhabit the shelter began to thaw as people became more friendly toward each other. Eventually Fred and his family were able to move out of the shelter, but Fred still went down to the shelter and talked with the people, helping them adjust to being there and assisting them to get back on their feet.

That's still another way we can serve others.

We could go on with story after story, but you get the picture. Of course, as I said, there is no guarantee that if we act in those ways toward others that they will change as the people in these true examples did. But these stories make the point that if we serve Jesus by serving others, it creates opportunities for miracles to happen, in us as well as others.

This is not hard to understand. It is just hard to do.

To be a servant, we give up our agenda to gain personal success and advancement at the expense of others. Instead, we commit ourselves to the welfare of others and wait for God to lead us as we give what we can to the needs of others.

It is a cold and lonely world when all people are looking out for themselves. It is a warmer and friendlier world when we look out for each other at home, at work, in our neighborhood, and in our church. As we follow Jesus's teaching and choose to serve Him by serving others, we demonstrate Christian servanthood.

SO, DON'T SINK YOUR OWN SHIP.

BE A SERVANT TO OTHERS.

CHAPTER REVIEW

Repetition is the key to mental ownership.

We are created by God to serve others.

1. The Bible teaches that Christians especially are to have a
    s_____ heart and serve one another.
2. We can serve by doing *what we can* to meet the n_____
    of others.

 DON'T SINK YOUR OWN SHIP

If something is important, you must repeat it until it changes you.

Chapter Summaries

1. Look to God for h_____.
2. R_____ q_____ when you sin.
3. Be totally o_____ to God.
4. Be a good s_____ of life's resources.
5. Be a s_____ to others.

 LIFE-CHECK

*Answer these questions, either individually by journaling the answer or
in a spiritual accountability group.*

1. Why do you think more people aren't inclined to "look out
    for the other person"? What prevents all of society from
    looking out for each other? What prevents churches from
    functioning that way? Do you see a solution, at least within
    our churches?
2. How do you think the world would be different if all people
    in authority used their authority only for the welfare of those
    under them? In the relationships in which you have authority,

do you consistently use your authority for the good of those
under you?

3. Where do you think we should draw the line, not only in
money but in time and emotional energy, between helping
others and meeting our own needs and the needs of those we
are responsible for?

 FOR FURTHER REFLECTION

Additional Scripture.

Matthew 5–7   Philippians 2:1–11

Mark 10:35–45   1 Peter 2:13–14

John 13:5   1 Peter 5:1–4

Ephesians 6:1–9

 RESOURCES

For further study.

30 Days to Growing in Your Faith (Chapter 16), Max Anders

Developing a Servant's Heart, Charles Stanley

A Gentle Answer, Scott Sauls

CHAPTER 6

CHOOSE THE FREEDOM OF SELF-DISCIPLINE

DON'T SINK YOUR OWN SHIP.
CHOOSE THE FREEDOM OF SELF-DISCIPLINE.

To be free to sail the seven seas, we must make ourselves a slave to the compass.

I strictly discipline my body and make it my slave, so that, after I have preached to others, I myself will not be disqualified.
—1 CORINTHIANS 9:27

I'll always remember when I was in high school how surprised I was the very first time I ever tried to hit a golf ball. I fully expected to feel a solid "thunk" and watch the ball trace a great rooster tail in the sky as it flew hundreds of yards down the manicured fairway. Instead, I didn't even hit it. I reared back like a Neanderthal attacking a snake and swung with undisguised fury. I wanted, and fully expected, to hear gasps of admiration as my friends watched the ball surge eagerly into the bright summer sky.

Instead, there was an angry "whooshing" sound. No "thunk." I felt a slight twinge in my lower back. Instead of gasps of admiration, there were tentative snorts of derision. In a thinly disguised attempt to make it look as if I had taken a practice swing, I quickly swung several more times, trying to replicate my original swing.

I approached the ball again, as one might approach a hornet's nest. What in the world had happened?!? That ball was supposed to go flying. Why didn't it? What do I do next time to make sure it does? I felt as though I were in the twilight zone, with unknown laws of physics taking over my life.

It was an unhappy situation. If I missed the ball again, there would be no pretense. I tried to not think about missing again, put my mind in neutral, and attacked again. This time, I hit it! However, instead of charging straight down the fairway, the ball sputtered off into the grass at a ninety-degree angle.

Welp, the jig was up. I now knew—and my friends knew—that I couldn't hit a golf ball. They compromised between sarcasm and sympathy, sniggering derisively but never actually saying anything. I claimed my mulligan (a free swing off the tee—not in the rules book) and tried again. This time, the ball dribbled pitifully down the fairway about a hundred feet (at least in the right direction this time). I then began a merciless assault on a dozen golf balls, alternating between losing them in the woods and cutting deep grins in their covers.

How could this happen to me? I had reasonable athletic skills. It looked so easy when I saw other people do it. If they could hit the ball down the fairway, why couldn't I? It was humiliating.

The memory of my golfing experience faded. Some years afterward, I decided I wanted to learn how to play the piano. So, I bought a book for adult learners and began practicing on a small electronic keyboard we had. It wasn't long before I realized that playing the piano was going to be much more difficult than I had ever imagined. After several months of practicing, anything I tried to play still sounded like a chimpanzee loose on the keyboard. I eventually decided that I was willing to give *whatever was in my power* to learn how to play the piano—*except* the amount of *time* required.

Sometime later, I determined that I wanted to learn how to paint with watercolors. So, for my birthday, my wife gave me a six-week adult education course of watercolor lessons at a nearby university. I was realistic, I thought. I didn't expect to be good when I started, but I didn't expect to be pathetic.

I was pathetic!

Everything I painted looked like a storm at sea. Try to paint a rose? It looked like a storm at sea. Try to paint a cardinal in a pine tree? It looked like a storm at sea. Try to paint a sailboat at anchor? It looked like a storm at sea. My artistic skills had not improved noticeably since grade school.

It wasn't until about then that I began to see the connection among all these things and began to learn a gigantic lesson that has been reinforced countless times since: almost everything is difficult to do well. From the simplest task such as hitting a golf ball to playing a musical instrument to flying a jet fighter plane, if someone is *good* at a skill, it is because he or she has worked very hard at it. And to work long and hard at something requires discipline.

So, only by discipline do we ever get really good at anything.

Many people think that discipline is limiting and restraining. And so it is. But it is also liberating and enabling. On the other hand, many people think that total freedom is liberating and enabling. And so it is. But it, too, is also limiting and restraining.

Someone has said, "To be free to sail the seven seas, you must make yourself a slave to the compass."

Achieving our goals almost always comes down to choosing carefully our freedoms and bondages. If we choose one freedom, we get a corresponding bondage. If we choose a bondage, we get a corresponding freedom. For example, if we place ourselves in bondage to brushing our teeth every day, we have the corresponding freedom of no cavities. If we exercise the freedom of not brushing our teeth, we have the corresponding bondage of cavities.

What we cannot have is freedom from the toothbrush and freedom from cavities. That kind of total freedom does not exist, because all actions have consequences that cannot be avoided.

One of my seminary professors used to ask two fundamental questions of us over and over again: "What do you want out of life? Are you willing to pay the price?" Those were life-changing questions. They have guided me ever since.

1. The Bible teaches that self-discipline is a virtue that Christians must cultivate.

The Bible teaches that self-discipline is a v_____ that Christians must cultivate.

The Bible teaches that self-discipline is a virtue and is part of the fruit of the Spirit that we all ought to possess: love, joy, peace, patience, kindness, goodness, faithfulness, gentleness, and self-control (Galatians 5:22–23).

Let's look at some additional passages that teach the virtue of discipline:

- "Don't you realize that in a race everyone runs, but only one person gets the prize? So run to win! All athletes are disciplined in their training. They do it to win a prize that will fade away, but we do it for an eternal prize. So I run with purpose in every step. I am not just shadowboxing. I discipline my body like an athlete, training it to do what it should" (1 Corinthians 9:24–27 NLT).
- "One who is slow to anger is better than the mighty, and one who rules his spirit, than one who captures a city" (Proverbs 16:32).
- "In your . . . knowledge . . . supply self-control" (2 Peter 1:6).

- Jesus taught that we should be faithful to use wisely the resources God gives us (Matthew 25:26–27).

So, we see throughout the Bible that self-discipline is a virtue we should all possess.

Of course, none of us are totally disciplined or totally undisciplined. And we are likely more disciplined in some areas than others. But, overall, the Bible teaches that discipline is a virtue and lack of discipline is a liability. The less disciplined we are, the more we pay the cause/effect price.

2. Each of us can become more self-disciplined.

Each of us can become m_____ self-disciplined.

Some of us are naturally more self-disciplined than others. Some of us also had self-discipline nurtured in us by our family, which encouraged our natural level of discipline—and some did not. So, for some of us the need for self-discipline is more acute than for others. Many, however, would admit to the need or desire for greater self-discipline.

Developing more self-discipline, however, is not an exact science. In fact, some ways are better for some people, and other ways are better for other people. In spite of this, there are some widely recognized strategies that are helpful.

For Christians, developing more self-discipline is a symbiotic relationship between us and the Holy Spirit. Philippians 2:12–13 says, ". . . work out your own salvation with fear and trembling; for it is God who is at work in you, both to desire and to work for *His* good pleasure."

This passage tells us that the Holy Spirit works in us for God's good pleasure, and we respond. God works—we respond. That is the process of spiritual growth. We cannot grow unless God works in us, but when God works in us we must respond. Growth does not come to the passive, but to those who respond to God's work in their lives.

So, like many things in life, we grow by doing as well as we can at the time, looking to God to strengthen us to do more. As in the gym, we get stronger by lifting light weights, which strengthens us to lift medium weights, which strengthens us to lift heavy weights.

3. Deciding to become more self-disciplined is a powerful first step.

D_____ to become more self-disciplined is a powerful first step.

The importance of making this decision to increase your self-discipline cannot be overstated. However, science as well as observation suggest that willpower has serious limitations in and of itself. It is more helpful to focus on the goal rather than trying to simply manufacture self-discipline. By concentrating on the prize, we are more likely to maintain the self-discipline necessary to reach the goal.

Olympic gold medalist Mary Lou Retton was once asked if she ever had thought about quitting before she got to the Olympics. She replied, "Oh, yes. Many times. But then when I realized it would be the death of my dreams, I always kept going." Again, desire was the root of self-discipline.

Lee Iacocca, the Ford auto executive who developed the iconic Ford Mustang, once said, "You've got to say, 'I think that if I keep working at this and want it badly enough, I can have it.' It's called perseverance!"

Finally, Olympic gold medalist Jesse Owens remarked, "We all have dreams. But in order to make dreams come into reality, it takes self-discipline."

So, the task is to concentrate on the dream. That's what feeds self-discipline.

4. Research gives us powerful insight into self-discipline.

R_____ gives us powerful insight into self-discipline.

Becoming more disciplined is not merely wishful thinking or a matter of subjective assessment. Science has given a great deal of attention to the subject of discipline, and can be extremely helpful in helping us make progress.

    a. There is a biological connection with self-discipline.
       1. The brain is like a muscle and can be strengthened to be more self-disciplined.
       2. Willpower can be depleted, so protect yourself from tempting friends, circumstances, activities, and locations.
       3. Clutter discourages discipline.
    b. Willpower is not the same as self-discipline. For most people, the problem is not a lack of discipline but a lack of vision. Being clear on the goal increases discipline to achieve the goal.
    c. Discipline in one area equals freedom in another.
    d. Designing the optimal environment for discipline is more than half the battle. Create an environment that is free of clutter, distractions, and obvious temptations.
    e. Helpful routines encourage self-discipline.[1]

Beyond these practical results of research into self-discipline, neurological research tells us that we can strengthen a desire, vision, or goal by repeating it over and over. Our brain does not necessarily believe what is true. It often believes what it is told most frequently. So, if we do not continually reinforce in our brain what our vision for our life is, that vision gets drowned out by the chorus of lies and distractions that modern culture provides over and over every day.

As a result, our vision fades, and so does our self-discipline.

To offset the eroding power of modern culture we can reinforce our vision continuously. When we do this, our vision is kept fresh and our self-discipline remains high.

5. Because God wants us to be more and more self-disciplined, we can pray.

Because God wants us to be more and more self-disciplined, we can p_____ .

God wants us to change. He wants us to develop greater self-discipline. The Holy Spirit's ministry is to illumine our minds to the truth of Scripture (1 Corinthians 2:10–13), convict us of sin and call us to righteousness (John 16:8), and build into us the fruit of the Spirit (Galatians 5:22–23). Since this is God's desire for us, how eager God must be to have us come to Him in prayer, asking for Him to work in our hearts and minds to give us increasingly greater self-discipline! Indeed, 1 John 5:14–15 teaches this very thing: "We are confident that he hears us whenever we ask for anything that pleases him. And since we know he hears us when we make our requests, we also know that he will give us what we ask for" (NLT).

We must be patient. As someone once said, "You can't be holy in a hurry." It will take time.

We must also be tenacious. We will slip often. But when we do, we get up again.

We *can* change. We *can be* more disciplined. And we can begin now. We have much to gain if we do.

SO, DON'T SINK YOUR OWN SHIP.
CHOOSE THE FREEDOM OF SELF-DISCIPLINE.

CHAPTER REVIEW

Repetition is the key to mental ownership.

To be free to sail the seven seas, we must make ourselves a slave to the compass.

1. The Bible teaches that self-discipline is a v_____ that Christians must cultivate.
2. Each of us can become m_____ self-disciplined.
3. D_____ to become more self-disciplined is a powerful first step.
4. R_____ gives us powerful insight into self-discipline.
5. Because God wants us to be more and more self-disciplined, we can p_____.

 DON'T SINK YOUR OWN SHIP

If something is important, you must repeat it until it changes you.

Chapter Summaries
1. Look to God for h_____.
2. R_____ q_____ when you sin.
3. Be totally o_____ to God.
4. Be a good s_____ of life's resources.
5. Be a s_____ to others.
6. Choose the f_____ of self-discipline.

 LIFE-CHECK

Answer these questions, either individually by journaling the answer or in a spiritual accountability group.

1. What do you want out of life? Are you willing to pay the price?

2. More specifically, what limitations do you currently have because you have taken the wrong freedoms? What freedoms do you currently have because you have taken the right limitations?

3. What freedoms do you not have that you would like to have? What limitations will you have to impose on yourself to get them?

4. What core values do you want to govern your life?

 FOR FURTHER REFLECTION

Additional Scripture.

Proverbs 16:32 Galatians 5:22–23
1 Corinthians 9:24–25 2 Peter 1:5–7

 RESOURCES

For further study.

30 Days to Growing in Your Faith (Chapter 15), Max Anders
The Science of Self-Discipline, Peter Hollins
Take the Stairs, Rory Vaden
The 7 Habits of Highly Effective People, Stephen Covey

CHAPTER 7

DON'T LET MOLEHILLS BECOME MOUNTAINS

Don't sink your own ship.
Don't let molehills become mountains.

If you let it, the small stuff in life will build up to become big stuff.

The one who is faithful in a very little thing is also faithful
in much.

—LUKE 16:10

I remember the night the bed fell.

I had flown to Chicago on a Friday to conduct an all-day seminar in a church the next day. It was wintertime and I felt like I was coming down with a nasty cold. I was getting a sore throat and a mild fever. I hate colds, anyway, and to have to give an all-day seminar with one was something I did not want to do. I had learned that my only hope was to take a bunch of vitamin C and get rest. I checked into the hotel, ate an early dinner, went to my room, and began getting ready for bed early at about 8:30. I wanted lights out by 9:00 p.m. Up by 7:00 a.m. would give me ten hours of sleep, and that just might help me avert a nasty, hacking cold.

Just about then I noticed all the noise out in the hall. Kids, thousands of them, rushing up and down the hallway like lemmings to the sea, making enough noise to raise the dead. "What in the world?!?" I wondered.

I stood in my doorway glaring at them, hoping that my stern demeanor would reduce them to silence. It didn't work. They didn't even see me. TVs were blaring from open doors and kids were shouting from one end of the hall to the other. There was a small soccer game going on three doors down. It was like Times Square on New Year's Eve, only with little people.

They say that when you have a brush with death, your whole life flashes in front of you. Well, in that moment my whole evening flashed in front of me: I knew I would get no sleep! But I tried anyway. Better to light a candle than curse the darkness. I called the manager, saying, "Could you please send someone up to my floor to try to quiet these kids down? I'm not feeling well, and I have a big day tomorrow, etc."

"Of course, Mr. Anders, we'll have somebody up there right away."

A half an hour later, "lights out" time, it was even noisier. I called the manager again.

"The noise is as bad as ever. Did you send anyone up?"

"Yes, Mr. Anders, but I'm afraid there are not enough adults to supervise the kids, and it apparently didn't do any good."

"Well, could you move me to another part of the hotel?"

This was a big hotel, and I could get away from the noise on another floor or wing.

"I'm sorry, Mr. Anders, there is a regional YMCA swim meet here in Chicago this weekend, and all the kids are staying here. The entire hotel is booked with swimmers."

I must have been the only non-YMCAer in the building. My encroaching illness made me desperate. I wanted to walk out in the hall and scream, "Be quiet, you little monsters! I need some sleep!" Three things kept me from doing this:

- First was the dim realization that total abandonment of restraint was a sin.
- Second was the thought that someone on the floor might end up at my seminar the next day.
- Third was a great wave of hopelessness that the kids would even hear me.

9:30 p.m.: I was getting more desperate. "I shouldn't get this upset," I thought to myself. "It's only working against me. I need to relax." This was a nice hotel, and the shower was extra large and enclosed in glass so that I could turn on a nozzle and fill it with steam. It was a personal sauna. "I'll get in the sauna for a while," I thought. "That will relax me."

I steamed myself into a wet noodle. I then groped my way back to bed, turned out the lights, and closed my eyes. Seconds later, they snapped open. I wasn't the least bit sleepy in spite of the fact that I had nearly boiled myself.

The bed had a coin-operated vibrator on it. That would help me—I'd get good and relaxed. Maybe I'd even go to sleep while it was running. I put *two* quarters in, just to be sure. All the time, the party was raging unabated outside my door. It's so hard to relax when you're uptight.

It was 10:00 p.m. by now. An hour's sleep had been lost. All I could think about was suffering through a horrible day tomorrow because those inconsiderate little no-brain monsters were allowed to run amok while the adults were down in the restaurant or bar or somewhere.

These were not very spiritual thoughts for someone who was going to spend the entire next day teaching the Bible.

My mental agitation plus the thorough cooking I had given myself earlier made the vibrator feel bad instead of good. Thirty seconds hadn't passed before I realized I had made a mistake. Oh, how I wished I had only put in *one* quarter instead of two!

I laid there trying to talk myself into relaxing. All this time, I was vibrating like a small air hammer. When my front teeth began to loosen, I finally flung the covers back and got up. I stormed over to a chair and sat there for another ten minutes until the vibrator finally shut off.

10:30 p.m.: I was debating between suicide and homicide when the thought occurred to me (why hadn't I realized this before?) that I often sleep when the television is on. I turned on the TV and flipped channels, looking for the best channel to sleep by. In an instant, I found it: a high school basketball game. The state of Illinois was having its championship game that night, and it was televised. Perfect! I sleep like a baby during sports events. I turned the game on just loud enough to help drown out the noise outside my door, but not so loud as to keep me from sleeping. Ah, finally, I had hit on the answer. It was late, but the night was not a total disaster. I could still get eight hours of sleep, my absolute minimum.

As I lay there trying to drift off, I heard a crazed announcer scream, "It's fifty-one to fifty-two. It's fifty-three to fifty-two. It's fifty-four to fifty-three. It's fifty-five to . . ." My eyes bugged—I couldn't help it. Though I was living in Atlanta at the time, I was born and raised in Indiana, the Hoosier state. The Basketball State. When you drive through the Midwest, you can tell how close you are to Indiana by how frequently you begin to see basketball backboards up on garages, barns, and light poles.

I found myself sitting on the end of the bed, wide-eyed at the spectacle before me. For reasons I will never understand, I somehow became "for" one of the teams, although I had never heard of either team before. Soon, I was shouting, "Go, Go, Go! Rebound! Defense! Shoot the ball!" In one of the most stunning victories I have ever witnessed, my team won by one point in the final second. It was exhilarating. There are few joys richer than a come-from-behind victory in basketball!

11:30 p.m.: The euphoria left as quickly as it had come. There was still noise outside my door, but it had slackened a little. I fell backward onto my bed, beside myself with frustration. I turned off the TV, turned out the lights, grabbed my pillow, and squeezed it around my ears. I flopped over on my stomach and bumped the headboard.

The headboard fell off the wall.

I was beginning to go numb. I put the headboard back on the wall, collapsed onto the bed, and

—the bed fell down!

Mattress, box spring, and frame, *all* buckled to the floor. Is this truly happening!?! By what unknown plot were all these events combining against me?!? Was I the focus of some secret conspiracy? With zombie-like mechanicalness, I put the bed back together.

12:00 a.m.: No noise outside. I was asleep in seconds.

I got up at 7:00 a.m. The hallway was silent as a tomb. The little rascals would be able to sleep until noon. After I got ready to go down for breakfast, I had to fight the impulse to crank the television to its loudest volume, leave my door open, and sing "She'll be comin' 'round the mountain when she comes!" at the top of my lungs, banging on all the doors as I left.

The interesting thing is . . . I was *not* sick. My only problem was the guilt that I had as I drove to the church to teach people the Bible on how to be a good Christian. I hadn't been a very good example. None of *them* knew it, of course, but *the Lord* did. And *so did I.* He and I had a talk to get things right before I reached the church.

It wouldn't have been a disaster if I *had* been sick that day. But I treated it as though it would have been, and when one thing after another just kept coming at me, I alternated between being a basket case and a time bomb. I couldn't decide whether to fall apart or blow up. When I look back on it, like many other things in life, it's funny now. But I wasn't laughing at the time.

The Bible speaks clearly to such things. In 1 Peter 2:19–21 we read, "For this *finds* favor, if for the sake of conscience toward God a person endures grief when suffering unjustly. For what credit is there if, when you sin and are harshly treated, you endure it with patience? But if when you do what is right and suffer *for it* you patiently endure it, this *finds* favor with God. For you have been called for this purpose, because Christ also suffered for you, leaving you an example, so that you would follow in His steps . . ."

This passage most directly relates to big things in life. But if so, how much more would it apply to little things? What are the little things that are accumulating in your life until they are in danger of becoming a big thing?

1. There are vital steps we can take to conquer molehills before they become mountains.

There are vital steps we can take to conquer m_____ before they become m_____.

How do we take it like Jesus would when the little problems of life mount up to become a big thing? Not being an expert on doing it right all the time (as witnessed by my lamentable personal examples), I do, however, try to learn from my mistakes. So, I would like to offer seven principles I have learned on how to stop molehills from becoming mountains:

1. *Differentiate between what is a big thing and what is a little thing.* We often treat little things as big things, and trouble mounts up before it really needs to. There aren't many big things in life. Life, death, health, food, clothing, shelter, relationships—these are some of the big things. Most of the other things are little things. If we admit they are little things, they don't weigh so much and don't add up so fast.

2. *Take comfort in the fact that "all things . . . work together for good to those who love God, to those who are called according*

to His purpose" (Romans 8:28). Not everything is good. But God will use everything for good, and we can take comfort in that.

3. *Learn to let go.* What does it really matter if I lose a little sleep? What does it matter if I get a nasty cold? What does it matter if a coworker treats me disrespectfully? An eternal perspective works wonders. A hundred years from now, what will it matter? When we put things into perspective, we can let go of the little things. These little things weigh us down only because we hold onto them.

4. *Understand the price we pay for little things becoming big things.* Because little things are *going* to happen, we are vulnerable to whatever little thing comes along unless we learn to let them go. We become like a leaf in the wind, helpless to the gusts of little things. Benjamin Franklin said, "Do not get angry at things common or unavoidable." It's a biblical principle stated in a helpful way. If we can become clear-eyed about the price we pay if we do not let little things go, this can keep us from being a slave to them.

5. *Decide ahead of time that you will not let the little things get you down.* Traffic in Atlanta, where I used to live years ago, used to drive me nuts. I drove about an hour to get to work, and it was stop-and-go much of the time with drivers often doing foolish and dangerous things to try to make better progress. I often took it personally, and would arrive at work a tense ball of nerves. Then I would sit down and try to write devotional material from the Bible about how to live the Christian life. I often thought to myself, *This is not right.*

So I finally decided that I would try to minister to people as I drove to work. I would look for opportunities to let people in front of me. I would wave at them as they often waved thankfully to me. I would deliberately slow down when I saw that someone needed to get in line, so the car could pull in ahead of me. When people merged from an on-ramp, I was the good Samaritan. I thought if I could appear overtly friendly on the road, I might encourage others to do the same. I might be the instigator of a great freeway revival in Atlanta. Sadly, this did nothing to improve the traffic in Atlanta, but it did transform my driving habits as well as my emotional state.

6. *Give others a break.* Others are often plagued by little things that become big things, and they are ready to lash out at us even though they don't really mean it. They, themselves, are hurting. I once read, "We ought always to be kind to others, for they may be walking life's road wounded." I thought of how many times I had been unkind to others in my pre-Christian days, not because I wanted to be unkind but because I was walking life's road wounded. It was a balm of healing when someone was kind to me. I decided I could be a balm of healing to others by being kind to them.

7. *Finally, and most importantly, memorize Scripture in areas of your weakness and review these passages over and over.* Also, pray. By sending truth through our minds over and over, and through prayer, the Holy Spirit can lift us to levels of patience we will not otherwise know.

2. When we revert, we simply repent and start over.

When we revert, we simply r_____ and start over.

Unfortunately, even when we've come to grips with this principle on an intellectual level, we still may not perform perfectly. I said I had mastered the frustration of bad traffic, and yet one day I faltered.

I was entering the freeway on my way home from a hard day at the church I was pastoring at the time. It was Friday afternoon, and I was tired, hungry, and had a slight headache. As I accelerated to merge into highway traffic, I didn't get up to speed as quickly as I might have. A BMW came flying up behind me, got within a foot of my bumper, and laid on the horn.

Instantly, I was livid. First, he was driving way too fast. Second, he had plenty of time to slow down. He did not have to ride my bumper the way he did—I was going the speed limit shortly after he started blowing his horn. Third, he didn't just toot; he laid on the horn. In what, for a pastor, would qualify as a nearsighted rage (it wasn't quite a blind rage), I slowed my Suburban to force him to pass me. When he did pass, I gunned the accelerator and got right up on *his* bumper. My heart pounded with adrenaline. Acid poured into my stomach. My jaws clenched reflexively. I would see how he liked being tailgated by a vehicle twice his size and half his cost!

Now . . . there are several things wrong with this picture.

First, it is sin to be so angry and respond the way I did. It was raw sin—it can't be called anything else. Second, it was very danger-ous: I could easily have caused a serious accident. Third, this person might have been a psychopath carrying a gun, and he could have shot me. Finally—this reason hit me the hardest—he might have attended my church! People in our church drove BMW's. Suddenly, I was buried with shame and guilt. I began to envision what I would say greeting him after church the next Sunday when he mentioned recognizing me on the freeway that past Friday. Considering the shape I was in, like David who followed adultery with murder, I probably would have said I was just wanting to be sure he saw me so I could say "hello."

Not good!

I repented, took my foot of the accelerator, and returned to normal.

As I said earlier, I had made some good progress driving in bad traffic. But even when we take good steps to keep the little things in life from becoming big things, we might not execute perfectly. We could falter. We may revert. When this happens, we get back in touch with reality, we repent, and we return to our pre-falter state.

3. The real issue isn't the small things that happen, but how we respond to the small things.

The real issue isn't the small things that happen, but how we r_____ to the small things.

I am happy to say that these lamentable examples happened decades ago, and nothing similar has happened for some time. That is evidence that we can grow out of these character deficiencies. There is hope.

I want to close this chapter with a story that I think captures this spirit so well. I don't know if the story is true, but the point is a good one.

I heard one time of a man who was being interviewed by the vice president of personnel of a large corporation for a job that would be a tremendous professional advancement, as well as a major increase in salary. It was a delicate job, however—one that would require judgment, patience, wisdom, and extraordinary people skills.

After going through all the normal interview procedures, the vice president of personnel took the candidate out to dinner. Unbeknownst to the candidate, the vice president had paid the waiters at the upscale restaurant to treat the man badly. They were too long in waiting on them. They brought the wrong order. They dumped soup in the man's lap. They charged too much. Through the whole ordeal, the man being interviewed took everything in stride.

After they left the restaurant, the vice president said, "You have the job if you want it." The man being interviewed was a little puzzled. It seemed like such an odd time to tell him. The vice president's response was, "You obviously had all the professional skills and experience for the position. We knew that before you came. The last thing we needed to know was how you would respond under pressure in dealing with people. The meal tonight was a test. We paid those waiters to treat you badly and eventually dump soup in your lap. If you had gotten angry or flustered or handled that situation poorly, you would not have gotten the job. You handled it well. The job is yours."

In life, when soup gets dumped in our lap, the soup isn't the issue. It is how we will respond to the soup. Scripture is clear on such things:

- Romans 8:28—" . . . all things . . . work together for good to those who love God . . ." Even the little things are under God's sovereignty.
- 1 Peter 2:19—" . . . this *finds* favor, if for the sake of conscience toward God a person endures grief when suffering unjustly." Whether in little or big things, God calls us to be patient and enduring.
- Luke 16:10—"The one who is faithful in a very little thing is also faithful in much . . ." God is a God of small things as well as big.

God is waiting to see how we handle little things . . . whether or not we let them build up to become big things. It is a test which, if we pass, several things happen:

- Our blood pressure is lower.
- We are spared the sometimes terrible cause/effect consequences of letting little things become big things and acting badly.
- We are given greater maturity, greater stability, greater strength, and greater peace.

- We get "promoted" to greater spiritual power and usefulness to God.

When small things build up, we need to let them go before they become big things.

So, DON'T SINK YOUR OWN SHIP.
DON'T LET MOLEHILLS BECOME MOUNTAINS.

CHAPTER REVIEW

Repetition is the key to mental ownership.

If you let it, the small stuff in life will build up to become big stuff.

1. There are vital steps we can take to conquer m_____ before they become m_____.
2. When we revert, we simply r_____ and start over.
3. The real issue isn't the small things that happen, but how we r_____ to the small things.

 DON'T SINK YOUR OWN SHIP

If something is important, you must repeat it until it changes you.

Chapter Summaries

1. Look to God for h_____.
2. R_____ q_____ when you sin.
3. Be totally o_____ to God.
4. Be a good s_____ of life's resources.
5. Be a s_____ to others.
6. Choose the f_____ of self-discipline.
7. Don't let m_____ become m_____.

LIFE-CHECK

Answer these questions, either individually by journaling the answer or in a spiritual accountability group.

1. What are some of the little things (such as traffic jams, the children, or relatives) that consistently build up to become big things in your life?
2. What do you think you can do to begin to let go of the little things?

3. Do you have trouble dealing with guilt over your failures? How do you think you can keep the guilt from becoming part of the burden?
4. What are your ideas on how you can turn an irritation into an opportunity to minister?

 FOR FURTHER REFLECTION

Additional Scripture.
> Matthew 6:31–33
> Romans 8:28
> 1 Peter 2:19–21

 RESOURCE

For further study.
> *30 Days to Growing in Your Faith* (Chapter 23), Max Anders

CHAPTER 8

GUARD YOUR MIND TO GUIDE YOUR LIFE

Don't sink your own ship.
Guard your mind to guide your life.

We become what we think about.

The good person out of the good treasure of his heart brings
forth what is good; and the evil person out of the evil treasure
brings forth what is evil; for his mouth speaks from that which
fills his heart.

—LUKE 6:45

I have a friend who has a nearly photographic memory. He used
to perform in Shakespearean plays, and to memorize his part
all he had to do was read through the play four or five times. Not
only did he have *his* part memorized, but he had *everyone's* part
memorized. He never seems to forget anything. Don't play *Trivial
Pursuit* with him!

This pales in comparison, however, to some other remarkable
feats of memory. Renowned conductor Arturo Toscanini had a
phenomenal memory and had memorized many complete musical

scores—the huge books of music the conductor uses when he conducts a symphony orchestra. It has every note played by every musical instrument in the orchestra! The conductor's score for Beethoven's Fifth Symphony is over 200 pages long!

Once, just before a concert, a clarinetist rushed up to Toscanini. "Maestro, Maestro! What am I to do? The E-flat key on my clarinet has just broken." Toscanini stared at him silently. The unnerved musician thought that perhaps the conductor was preparing to murder him. Instead, after a long moment, Toscanini's trance-like stare was broken and he said, "That is all right. You don't have an E-flat tonight."

But as intriguing and intricate as the mind's capacity for memory is, even more powerful is the mind's impact on our behavior. Luke 6:45 reads, "The good person out of the good treasure of his heart brings forth what is good; and the evil person out of the evil treasure brings forth what is evil. For his mouth speaks from that which fills his heart."

Both Scripture and observation tell us that we must be careful what we let into our minds and what we allow our minds to dwell on, for that is what produces our words and actions.

1. In many ways, the mind works just like a computer.

In many ways, the mind works just like a c_____.

You only get out of something what you put into it—garbage in, garbage out. The same is generally true of our minds. If we put worthless, inaccurate, or faulty information into our minds, that is what we tend to get out of it.

Unlike computers, however, the mind can create its own worthless, inaccurate, or faulty information. Garbage doesn't have to be downloaded from the outside. Someone can tell us as a child that we are stupid, and afterward we will continue to water, fertilize, and nurture that seedling into a forest of negative thoughts and emotions.

That is why it is so critical that we exercise great care in what we allow into our minds and what we allow our minds to dwell on.

2. As Christians, we must believe what is true, fill our minds with truth, and repeat truth until it changes us.

As Christians, we must b_____ what is true, f_____ our minds with truth, and r_____ truth until it changes us.

First, we must believe what is true.

We have to be diligent, discerning, and honest to make sure that we are not ignorant or self-deceived. It does no one any good not to be in touch with reality.

In her book titled *Up to No Good: The Rascally Things Boys Do*, Kitty Harmon recounts true stories of men who grew up to be "perfectly decent." I've retold one particular story from her book before, but do so again because it is such a powerful illustration of a truth worth reminding ourselves of.

In one story, "Lou was playing with some friends and decided to try flying. So, they climbed up onto the roof of the barn, and Lou strapped some heavy wooden boards onto his brother's arms. Then they counted down, and he jumped. He was lying on the ground, groaning in pain with several broken bones, and Lou yelled, 'Hey Shorty! You forgot to flap your wings!'"[1]

You see, Lou's brother, Shorty—momentarily persuaded by Lou—*believed* he could fly. Based on that belief, Shorty jumped off the roof of the barn. But what he believed was wrong, and he paid the price.

That's what can happen if you are not in touch with reality.

So, step number one is to work hard to make sure that what you believe is actually true.

Second, *we need to fill our minds with truth.*

The more truth we know, the better off we are.

I remember as a small boy not knowing what poison ivy looked like. I got into some and paid a painful price for a miserable couple of weeks. Now I know what it looks like and I haven't had it since. A little knowledge can go a long way.

We need to be alert to, on the hunt for, and highly regard what is true. Jesus said, "You will know the truth, and the truth will set you free" (John 8:32). To the degree that we do not know the truth, or to the degree that we do not believe it, we are vulnerable to ignorance and deception.

Being thick-headed about truth is not an advantage.

Third, *we have to repeat truth until it changes us.*

How many times have you heard something that was true . . . and you recognized it as important . . . and you let it go in one ear and out the other? A million, perhaps?

Just hearing something doesn't mean we "own" it. If something is true, we have to repeat it until it changes us.

We must take great care because, as I said, what we put into our minds determines who we become. That is why the Scriptures make a clear connection between our thoughts and our actions:

- Proverbs 23:7 says, "For as he thinks within himself, so he is."
- Luke 6:45 reads, "A good man out of the good treasure of his heart brings forth good; and an evil man out of the evil treasure of his heart brings forth evil. For out of the abundance of the heart his mouth speaks."
- Romans 12:2 says, "Do not be conformed to this world, but be transformed by the renewing of your mind, so that you may prove what the will of God is, that which is good and acceptable and perfect."

3. As Christians, we must guard our minds against false teaching, temptations, and spiritual deceptions.

As Christians, we must guard our minds against false t_____, t_____, and spiritual d_____.

First, *we have to guard our minds against false teaching.*

We need to watch out for doctrinal errors that can divert us from the true gospel. Scripture encourages us to "contend earnestly for the faith that was once for all time handed down to the saints" (Jude 1:3). God's revelation to us was delivered once and for all. That means nothing is going to be added to it.

And that means the message has been around for a while. As someone has said, "If it's new, it's not true"—because the biblical faith we believe is the one that was handed down from "the saints" two thousand years ago.

How do we guard our minds against false teachings? By comparing what we are hearing with the Bible and with traditional interpretations, and being wary of something new. Of course there have always been doctrinal differences in the church, but such differences have been clearly defined, well-reasoned, and "known" for hundreds of years.

The internet makes it possible for false teachers to have a loud voice. If a Christian is not already biblically well-taught, he or she can be vulnerable to being led astray. Thus, believers should find reputable teachers who have earned trust over sufficient time and be on guard against false teachers.

Second, *we must guard our minds against temptations.*

Psalm 101:3 says, "I will set no worthless thing before my eyes."

If we're going to guard our minds, we have to be careful about what we watch on television and movies, what we listen to, what we read, what we engage in on the internet and social media, and what games we play.

The Bible says very clearly in James 1:14 that sin starts with a thought. You've probably heard the old American proverb: "You sow a thought, you reap an action. You sow an action, you reap a habit. You sow a habit, you reap a destiny."

The same is true, of course, about more than television. Almost anything electronic is fraught with inherent dangers, to say nothing of questionable friends, places, activities, etc.

Our destiny begins in our thoughts. The mind is a strategic battlefield, and if Satan can get your thought life, he's going to get you. So those harmless thoughts are not harmless at all. Guard your mind against temptation.

Finally, *we must guard our minds against spiritual deception.*

Satan is the author of deception. In John 8:44, Jesus said that Satan is "a liar and the father of lies."

First John 4:1 says, "do not believe every spirit, but test the spirits to see whether they are from God, because many false prophets have gone out into the world." The Bible says that the devil disguises himself as an angel of light (2 Corinthians 11:14). He is intensely interested in trying to deceive Christians. We must be alert to that danger.

4. As Christians, we must guard what we let into our minds, what we let our minds create, and what we let our minds dwell on.

As Christians, we must guard what we let i_____ our minds, what we let our minds c_____, and what we let our minds d_____ on.

First, *we must guard what we let into our minds.*

You've seen the old magician's trick where he puts a silk handkerchief in a top hat and then, presto, pulls out a rabbit. What he gets out is not the same as what he put in. Well, that's a trick, and it's not true. You can only get out of something what you put into it.

As we have said, the same is true with the mind. You get out of it what you put into it. So, if we want good and helpful things out of our minds, we must put good and helpful things into our minds. If we put bad and unhelpful things into our minds and then go to our minds later for good and helpful things, it doesn't work. So, we have to guard what we let into our minds.

Second, *we must guard what we let our minds create.*

Our minds are affected not only by what we put into them but also by what we let them create. When we exercise our imagination, we are creating things mentally that can be just as good or just as bad as letting things into our minds.

For example, someone asked Thomas Edison how he ever came up with the idea for the electric light bulb. He said, "By thinking about it all the time." He let his mind dwell on ideas for the electric light bulb and thus helped change the course of history. That is an example of something good that can happen when we let our minds create good things. The same is true with bad things.

The same is also true spiritually. We can create both good and bad thoughts.

Finally, *we must guard what we let our minds dwell on.*

Finally, we need to be careful about letting our minds dwell on bad or negative thoughts. Philippians 4:8 says, "Whatever is true, whatever is honorable, whatever is right, whatever is pure, whatever is lovely, whatever is of good repute, if there is any excellence and if anything worthy of praise, dwell on these things."

Why? Because if we dwell on things that are not true, if we dwell on things that are wrong, if we dwell on hurts, if we dwell on anger or resentment, if we dwell on failure or other negative things, those things grow, dominate our thinking, and affect our emotions. They begin to control who we are and what we do. But, on the other hand, if we dwell on positive things, then those positive things begin to dominate our thinking and affect our emotions and actions.

5. As Christians, we must guard our minds with Scripture and prayer.

As Christians, we must guard our minds with S_____ and p_____.

We must guard our minds with Scripture and prayer.

Regarding Scripture, in Matthew 4 we see Jesus resisting the temptations of the devil by quoting Scripture.

Regarding prayer, in Philippians 4:6–7 the apostle Paul wrote: "Do not be anxious about anything, but in everything by prayer and pleading with thanksgiving let your requests be made known to God. And the peace of God, which surpasses all comprehension, will *guard your hearts and minds* in Christ Jesus."

So, we see that both Scripture and prayer are powerful weapons against falsehood.

Conclusion

In order to live well, we must first think well. To that end, we must guard against false teaching, temptation, and spiritual deception. At the same time, we must guard what we let into our minds, what we let our minds create, and what we let our minds dwell on. And we must use Scripture and prayer as essential weapons.

As we use these truths to help us think well, the Lord will bless us and enable us to live well.

SO, DON'T SINK YOUR OWN SHIP.
GUARD YOUR MIND TO GUIDE YOUR LIFE.

CHAPTER REVIEW

Repetition is the key to mental ownership.

We become what we think about.

1. In many ways, the mind works just like a
   c_____.
2. As Christians, we must b_____ what is true, f_____
   our minds with truth, and r_____ truth until it
   changes us.
3. As Christians, we must guard our minds against false
   t_____, t_____, and spiritual
   d_____.
4. As Christians, we must guard what we let i_____ our
   minds, what we let our minds c_____, and what we let
   our minds d_____ on.
5. As Christians, we must guard our minds with
   S_____ and p_____.

DON'T SINK YOUR OWN SHIP

If something is important, you must repeat it until it changes you.

Chapter Summaries

1. Look to God for h_____.
2. R_____ q_____ when you sin.
3. Be totally o_____ to God.
4. Be a good s_____ of life's resources.
5. Be a s_____ to others.
6. Choose the f_____ of self-discipline.
7. Don't let m_____ become m_____.
8. G_____ your mind to g_____ your life.

LIFE-CHECK

Answer these questions, either individually by journaling the answer or in a spiritual accountability group.

1. On a scale of one to ten, how are you doing at guarding what you let into your mind? What is the area of your greatest weakness?

2. On the same scale, how are you doing at guarding what you allow your mind to dwell on? What is the area of your greatest weakness?

3. Finally, on the same scale, how well do your friends encourage you by their own example to follow the Lord?

 FOR FURTHER REFLECTION

Additional Scripture.

Proverbs 23:7   2 Corinthians 10:5
Luke 6:45   Philippians 4:8–9
Romans 12:1–2

 RESOURCES

For further study.

30 Days to Growing in Your Faith (Chapters 6, 9), Max Anders
Change Your Heart, Change Your Life, Gary Smalley
Winning the War in Your Mind, Craig Groeschel

CHAPTER 9

USE YOUR TONGUE TO HELP, NOT TO HURT

DON'T SINK YOUR OWN SHIP.
USE YOUR TONGUE TO HELP, NOT TO HURT.

If we control the tongue, we control the whole person.

Let no unwholesome word come out of your mouth, but if there is any good word for edification according to the need of the moment, say that, so that it will give grace to those who hear.

—EPHESIANS 4:29

In high school, I thought I was a BMOC—Big Man On Campus. I was an athlete, played in several school bands, had the lead in the school play, and was invited to all the parties the cool kids had. I thought I was big stuff—on the outside. But inside I was insecure, uncertain, and easily intimidated. I was an overachiever simply because I had no confidence whatsoever in my inherent worth as a human being. So I had to rely on achievements to validate my worth as a member of the human race.

I would periodically do other things to validate my status, to remind myself and others that I was, in fact, a BMOC. However, these things were usually the actions of a JERK, which is often what I really was. But I didn't realize it at the time.

One of my most disheartening forays into JERK-dom happened when a new girl moved to our small town. She was quiet and shy, although I remember her being a nice young lady as I look back on everything many years after. She had a pleasant countenance and was polite, courteous, and a good student. There was nothing wrong with her.

But the ways of JERKs are difficult to fathom, and for some reason several of "the cool guys" singled this girl out for unwarranted attention. We used to talk about her within her hearing. We said nothing ugly, but just asked questions about where she came from, what she was like, and why she was so quiet. But it was especially rude because we did it within her hearing. However, she never said anything, never acknowledged our rudeness, and never lost the pleasant look on her face.

I remember that at one basketball game where the girl was sitting in front of us, we started blowing on the back of her head. We blew very slightly at first. We wanted her to feel her hand over the back of her head and wonder what was there. But she didn't. So we blew harder. She still didn't acknowledge our pestering. Finally, we blew so hard that we parted her hair down the back of her head. Yet she did nothing. She never acknowledged our presence and never lost the pleasant look on her face.

To this day, I don't fully understand why we did that. I was not a consciously mean kid. I think it had something to do with establishing my place over someone new so I could reassure myself of my standing in the flock, like chickens fighting for a position in the pecking order.

When I think of this now, I reproach myself for my thoughtless actions. How we must have hurt her! And it was for no reason. Yet she was the picture of grace through it all.

In reality, she was a BW(oman)OC. I was just a big JERK! I don't know where she is today, but I wish I could talk to her and ask her to forgive me. I wish I could tell her how much I regret my rudeness and how much I admire her for her graciousness.

1. The tongue is extremely powerful.

The tongue is extremely p_____.

You've heard the saying, "Sticks and stones may break my bones, but words will never hurt me." Of course, this is not true. Words can hurt—and words can heal. Words can tear down—and words can build up. Words can destroy—and words can create.

We have, behind our lips, a tool that gives us the ability to encourage, exalt, and empower—or discourage, damage, and defeat.

If we had a physical weapon this powerful, it would have to be licensed and registered with the authorities. Some people would not be permitted to carry it. Yet, here we are—everyone armed with a weapon so powerful that lives hang in the balance when we use it. And many of us don't know how to use it well.

2. The Bible commands us to use our tongues wisely.

The Bible commands us to use our tongues w_____.

The Bible teaches that the tongue is extremely powerful, and it commands us to use our tongues wisely.

God knows the power of the tongue. He gave it to us, and He instructed us on how to use it. The central passage in the Bible on the tongue is found in James 3:2–6:

> If anyone does not stumble in what he says, he is a perfect man, able to rein in the whole body as well. Now if we put the bits into the horses' mouths so that they will obey us, we direct their whole body as well. Look at the ships too; though they are so large and are driven by strong winds, they are nevertheless directed by a very small rudder wherever the inclination of the

pilot determines. So also the tongue is a small part of the body, and *yet* it boasts of great things.

See how great a forest is set aflame by such a small fire! And the tongue is a fire, the *very* world of unrighteousness; the tongue is set among our body's parts as that which defiles the whole body and sets on fire the course of *our* life, and is set on fire by hell.

Whew! Strong words. And that's not the end of it. The Bible has more to say about our words: "The good person out of the good treasure of his heart brings forth what is good; and the evil *person* out of the evil *treasure* brings forth what is evil; for his mouth speaks from that which fills his heart" (Luke 6:45).

What comes out of our mouths originates in our hearts. The heart is the reservoir; our words are merely the stream flowing out of it. How embarrassing! Everyone knows! They know our hearts by listening to our words!

However, changing our speech is not an easy task because it isn't merely our speech that needs change—it's our heart. That's why James wrote that if we could control the tongue, we could control the entire body. Therefore, we have to look honestly and accurately at our speech. Is it helpful speech or hurtful speech? No one speaks all of one and none of the other, but this must not keep us from being honest.

When we are honest about our speech, we can look at the characteristics of good speech and bad speech with the goal of improving our own. If we use our tongue wisely and well, it will honor God, improve our relationships with other people, and make our lives go better.

3. There are four ways we can use our tongues to hurt.

There are four ways we can use our tongues to h_____.

Lies

I remember my first conscious, bald-faced lie. I was five years old, and I had taken six cents from my piggy bank (which I was forbidden to do without permission) to buy candy from the little grocery store in our tiny town. I plunked down my coins, chose six pieces of penny candy, and lit out for the garden to hide. I was feeding contentedly on my illicit treasure when my brother found me and asked me where I got the money to buy the candy. I didn't think very far ahead at the age of five: I told him that our sister had given it to me. I thought that would be the end of it. How was I to know the Little Snitch was going to go straight to the house and get to the bottom of this whole thing?

Well, before I knew it, the Little Snitch came trotting back to my hiding place in the garden and announced that Mom wanted to talk to me. I was caught. I confessed to the whole sordid affair and was punished by having to stand in the corner for a year.

Lying is wrong for several reasons. First, it is a sin against God. Second, it is a sin against others. Third, it never pays in the long run. Sooner or later our lies catch up with us. People learn that we lie, and it ruins our reputation and our credibility. Proverbs 12:22 says, "Lying lips are an abomination to the LORD, but those who deal faithfully are His delight."

When a Christian lies, he is hurting God's reputation, hurting his own reputation, destroying relationships, and eroding his chances for success in life.

Anger

A second common form of hurtful speech is an angry outburst. How easy, how natural it is for us to fly off the handle or say something unkind out of anger!

A young boy once asked, "Dad, how do wars get started?"

His father replied, "Well, take the First World War. That got started when Germany invaded Belgium."

Immediately his wife interrupted him. "Tell the boy the truth. It began because somebody was murdered."

The husband stiffened and said, "Are you answering the question, or am I?"

The wife turned and left the room in a huff, slamming the door behind her. An uneasy silence settled over the room.

"Never mind, Dad," said the boy. "I think I know the answer."

The Bible says that everyone should be "quick to hear, slow to speak, *and* slow to anger; for a man's anger does not bring about the righteousness of God" (James 1:19–20).

How many times we get this turned *exactly* around—being slow to hear, quick to speak, and quick to get angry! But when we do this, we sin. We don't achieve the righteousness of God.

Gossip and Rumors

"Did you hear that Joe and Susan are having problems? It's terrible. Another woman, I think."

"Well, I'm not surprised. She's a compulsive perfectionist and drives *me* nuts. I'm glad *I'm* not married to her. Not that Joe's right, of course."

"Of course. But look what it's doing to the kids. They're both teenagers now and wilder than March hares."

"Yes. It's too bad. They really need our prayers."

How many times conversations such as this take place in the name of "information for more enlightened prayer," when it's nothing more than gossip! Gossip is "saying something negative about a person to someone who is not part of a solution."

Gossip is often tricky to avoid because it is so interesting and because our genuine interest and concern for others sometimes draw us into a deeper level of conversation about people than is appropriate. So we have to be on our guard. It is amazing how easily we can get drawn into gossip if we drop our guard!

Spreading rumors is a similar and equally illicit form of gossip. For instance, Paul rebuked people who had become "gossips" and "busybodies" due to their idleness (1 Timothy 5:13).

Both gossiping and rumor-spreading are using the tongue for harm.

Swearing

At one of the churches I pastored, a prominent lay leader and I were talking at a social function. I asked him how his job was going. He had, in outward appearance, a rather exciting profession. But his face clouded over and he leaned close to me, saying in a confidential whisper, "Oh, it's a @%#*!# pain!"

More than a little surprised, I wondered why he thought I would want to hear that language if it was unfit for the rest of the people in the room.

I have had similar experiences with people telling off-color jokes.

Vulgar and coarse speech is a growing problem among Christians in our time of cultural disintegration. We need to guard against it.

In the end the Bible says, "Let no unwholesome word come out of your mouth, but only such *a word* as is good for edification according to the need *of the moment*, so that it will give grace to those who hear" (Ephesians 4:29). Words of "edification" do not include lying, gossiping, angry outbursts, swearing, or telling dirty jokes. Again, the apostle Paul wrote: "*there must be no* filthiness or foolish talk, or vulgar joking, which are not fitting, but rather giving of thanks" (Ephesians 5:4). Rather, "Your speech must always be with grace, *as though* seasoned with salt, so that you will know how you should respond to each person" (Colossians 4:6).

Furthermore, James said, "If anyone thinks himself to be religious, yet does not bridle his tongue but deceives his *own* heart, this person's religion is worthless" (James 1:26). Strong words, but true. Motivated Christians must be serious and careful about how they use their tongues.

4. There are four ways we can use our tongues to help.

There are four ways we can use our tongues to h_____.

On the other hand, the power of the tongue for good is just as great as the power of the tongue for harm.

Encouragement

The power of encouragement is impressive. There are few things more powerful.

Encouragement can turn defeat into victory, sadness into joy, and despair into hope. Mark Twain once remarked that he could live for two months on a good compliment. John Maxwell said, "Everyone needs encouragement. And everyone who receives it—young or old, successful or less-than-successful, unknown or famous—is changed by it."

Studies have shown that children who receive encouragement from a teacher are significantly more likely to continue their education. Other studies have shown that workplace happiness skyrockets when employees receive encouragement from a boss.

Neuroscience has shown that positive words can actually change your brain, alter your genes, build resiliency, promote healthy mental function, and trigger the motivational centers of your brain.

Perhaps that's why the Bible says so much about encouragement:

- Anxiety in a person's heart weighs it down, but a good word makes it glad (Proverbs 12:25).
- Pleasant words are a honeycomb, sweet to the soul and healing to the bones (Proverbs 16:24).
- Let no unwholesome word come out of your mouth, but if there is any good word for edification according to the need of the moment, say that, so that it will give grace to those who hear (Ephesians 4:29).

Don't you love it when someone says something to encourage you? Well, that's how much others enjoy being encouraged by you.

Saying encouraging things to others is one of the most powerful ways we can use the tongue for good. What is more, like many positive attributes, encouragement not only helps those who hear it, but it helps those who speak it.

Truth in Love

Ephesians 4:15 teaches that we should be "speaking the truth in love." This can be hard to do. We have a great deal of trouble keeping our balance. We want to either speak the truth without love, or we want to speak love without truth.

But Proverbs says, "Better is open rebuke than love that is concealed. Faithful are the wounds of a friend, but deceitful are the kisses of an enemy" (27:5–6).

So we see that the duty of a loving friend is to tell someone the truth if it needs to be said.

Therefore, if someone comes to you with truth that is hard to hear, hearing it anyway is the right thing to do. Proverbs 15:31 says, "One whose ear listens to a life-giving rebuke will stay among the wise."

The key is that what we say must be truth, and it must be said in love.

Good Reports

One of the most uplifting things we can hear is when someone tells us something good someone said about us. Perhaps you are a parent, and your child's teacher has told you what a good student he or she is in math. Don't keep that information to yourself; share it with your child.

Suppose you hear someone say a person taught a really good Sunday school class. Go tell that person. A good report is a powerful way to say words that help.

A lot of good in the world can be *magnified* if we develop the simple habit of sharing with others something good that we see or hear about them.

Cheerfulness

Would you rather be around a cheerful person or a cheerless person? Unless you are highly unusual, you would rather be around a cheerful person. Why? Well, because they are so . . . cheerful.

Cheerfulness and contentment are great beautifiers, and are famous preservers of good looks.   —*Charles Dickens*

Cheerfulness can change misfortune into love and friends.
                                              —*Louisa May Alcott*

What sunshine is to flowers, smiles are to humanity. These are but trifles, to be sure; but scattered along life's pathway, the good they do is inconceivable.   —*Joseph Addison*

Negative people drag us down. Positive people lift us up. Cheerful people fill us with encouragement, hope, pleasure, and good will.

Even Scripture has a good deal to say about cheerfulness:

- A cheerful heart is good medicine, but a broken spirit saps a person's strength (Proverbs 17:22 NLT).
- This is the day the LORD has made. We will rejoice and be glad in it (Psalm 118:24 NLT).
- God loves a person who gives cheerfully (2 Corinthians 9:7 NLT).

Therefore, if we want to speak words that help, we should be cheerful. Cheerfulness makes life go better for us, as well as for those we are around.

Some people are, by nature, more positive than others. But all of us can be more positive than we might naturally be, just by making the decision to be. A world of good can open up to us if we accept the challenge to become a person whose words help and heal. Abraham Lincoln once said, "A person is about as happy as he makes up his mind to be." In the same way, a person's speech is about as helpful as he makes up his mind for it to be.

Become a person whose words help and heal. *Think about your speech. Do you lie (how about exaggerate)? Do you get angry? Do you gossip? Do you swear or use vulgar language? Are you true to your word? If you say something, can others count on its being true?*

On the other hand, do you encourage others? Do you tell the truth in love? Do you give good reports to others, and are you cheerful?

The Lord wants to clean your heart of hurtful speech. It is for your own good, as well as for the Lord's reputation, that your heart be cleaned up and your language reflect this cleansing.

Study your speech. Be honest with yourself. Ask the Holy Spirit to pinpoint your weaknesses and to strengthen you to overcome them. Then commit yourself to being a person whose words help, not hurt.

So, DON'T SINK YOUR OWN SHIP.
USE YOUR TONGUE TO HELP, NOT TO HURT.

CHAPTER REVIEW

Repetition is the key to mental ownership.

If we control the tongue, we control the whole person.

1. The tongue is extremely p_____.
2. The Bible commands us to use our tongues w_____.
3. There are four ways we can use our tongues to h_____.
4. There are four ways we can use our tongues to h_____.

 DON'T SINK YOUR OWN SHIP

If something is important, you must repeat it until it changes you.

Chapter Summaries

1. Look to God for h_____.
2. R_____ q_____ when you sin.
3. Be totally o_____ to God.
4. Be a good s_____ of life's resources.
5. Be a s_____ to others.
6. Choose the f_____ of self-discipline.
7. Don't let m_____ become m_____.
8. G_____ your mind to g_____ your life.
9. Use your tongue to h_____, not to h_____.

 LIFE-CHECK

Answer these questions, either individually by journaling the answer or in a spiritual accountability group.

1. How would you characterize your speech? Do you see yourself as someone who is known for helpful speech or hurtful speech?

2. If you are married, how do you think your spouse would characterize your speech? If you aren't married, how would your parents or good friends characterize your speech? Are you a person who is known for hurtful speech or helpful speech?

3. Of the hurtful speech characteristics in this chapter, which is your greatest weakness? How do you think you can begin to overcome that weakness?

4. Of the helpful speech characteristics in this chapter, which is your greatest strength? How do you think you can capitalize on it?

5. When you say something, are you consistently true to your word? If you are or are not, how do you think that impacts you?

 FOR FURTHER REFLECTION

Additional Scripture.

Proverbs 12:25	Ephesians 4:15
Proverbs 12:22	Ephesians 4:29
Proverbs 15:31	Ephesians 5:4
Proverbs 16:24	1 Timothy 5:13
Proverbs 27:5–6	James 1:19–20
Luke 6:45	James 3:2–6

 RESOURCES

For further study.

A Gentle Answer, Scott Sauls

Watch Your Mouth, Tony Evans

CHAPTER 10

TRUST GOD'S DEFINITION OF SUCCESS

DON'T SINK YOUR OWN SHIP.
TRUST GOD'S DEFINITION OF SUCCESS.

Success is being faithful to what God asks of us and leaving the results to Him.

This Book of the Law shall not depart from your mouth, but you shall meditate on it day and night, so that you may be careful to do according to all that is written in it; for then you will make your way prosperous, and then you will achieve success.
—JOSHUA 1:8

I have always been fascinated by dogsled racing. I'm not sure why. I think it has something to do with the stark do-or-die, winner-take-all circumstances and the almost mystical bond that develops between a musher (dogsled racer) and his dogs. So I read with unusual interest about author Gary Paulsen, a Minnesotan who ran the 1,200-mile Iditarod dogsled race from Anchorage to Nome, Alaska, in the dead of winter. He had never run a dogsled race and had put in only 150 training miles with his dog team in the familiar Minnesota woods.

In a fit of naivete bordering on insanity brought on after some amateur sledding one day, Paulsen decided to enter the race on a course that, he would later learn, would nearly kill him several times. He immediately started his team on endurance training, and the first day turned out to be a microcosm of his entire sledding career. When all the dogs were hitched to the sled, he went to the rig, stood by it, waved to his wife who was watching by the door of the house, and jerked the rope holding the sled to a tree. The dogs bolted.

> I don't think the rig hit the ground more than twice all the way across the yard. *My [word]*, I thought, *they've learned to fly*. With me hanging out the back like a tattered flag we came to the end of the driveway, where we would have to turn, must turn onto the road.
>
> The dogs made the turn fine.
>
> The rig started to as well, but I had forgotten to lean into the turn and it rolled . . . we set off down the road with the rig upside down, all the gear gone, and me dragging on the gravel on my face.
>
> It took me four miles to get the rig up on its wheels, by which time the pipe-handlebar I had welded into position was broken off and I had nothing to hang on to but the steering ropes. I was also nearly completely denuded, my clothes having been torn to shreds during the dragging.
>
> We did the thirty miles [of the training run] in just under two and a half hours and never once was I in anything like even partial control of the situation. . . .
>
> In subsequent runs I left the yard on my face, my [rear], my back, my belly. . . . I once left the yard with wooden matches in my pocket and had them ignite as I was being dragged past the door of the house, giving me the semblance of a meteorite,

screaming something about my [pants] being on fire at Ruth, who was laughing so hard she couldn't stand.[1]

Paulsen never gave up, though. He ran the two-week-long Iditarod race and finished. It was an astonishing feat! The training runs were a stroll in the park by comparison.

When Paulsen crossed the finish line, a reporter asked him if he had anything to say. He replied, "I'm coming back next year and winning." He did go back two years later—but he didn't win. He eventually wisely retired and lived as a writer in New Mexico.

Gary Paulsen never won the race he said he would win. Was he a failure because he didn't win? Or was he a success simply because he did his best? What is success, after all? Can you fail at the task and still succeed? And, for the Christian, how does God view success? Can we fail at the task and still succeed in God's eyes? Is it enough just to finish the course, or must we win?

1. Americans are preoccupied with success.

Americans are preoccupied with s_____.

Americans, preoccupied with success, often interpret it as being number one. Athletes shove their faces into the lenses of sideline cameras, hold up their index fingers, and shout, "We're number one!" Is that success?

Each year, *Forbes* magazine publishes the *Forbes* 400, a list of the four hundred richest individuals in the United States. Is that success? My *alma mater* sends out a regular mailing listing the achievements of its graduates, and there are many stories of her children having done well. Is that success?

Is it possible for everyone to succeed? How can we know when we have succeeded? For Americans in the twenty-first century, does success satisfy?

2. Success doesn't satisfy.

Success doesn't s_____.

Unfortunately, the modern American definition of success often doesn't satisfy, because after we have gotten what we want, we want something more. Someone has said, "We climb the ladder of success only to find it is leaning against the wrong wall." Proverbs 27:20 says that "Nor are the eyes of a person ever satisfied." The world's success is a carrot on a stick. When you take a step toward it, it moves. So you have to decide whether or not you are going to be the donkey.

I remember that when I first went to college not far from my small hometown, my vision for my life after I graduated from college was to move back to my hometown, live in some newly built apartments, and teach high school English. After a few years into college, I then wanted to go on to graduate school and return to teach college, living in some apartments near campus. But then I wanted a doctoral degree to be able to teach in seminary.

My life eventually changed course, and I went into the pastorate of a brand-new church, totally satisfied if it never grew. I just wanted to be faithful to the people God brought to us. But before long I became discouraged with the congregation's lack of growth. Later I pastored a larger church that experienced meteoric growth, but this didn't satisfy me either. I am a slow learner, but it finally dawned even on me that the finish line kept moving. The sad thing was that I was the one who moved it.

Needing to be a success is a deadly trap, and Satan will use it to discourage us, defeat us, and even destroy us if we let him. We must let go of the need to succeed from the world's perspective. It isn't necessarily wrong to desire success if it is for the right reasons, and it isn't wrong to work hard to achieve it. But when we *need* it, we're in trouble.

3. We typically desire success in order to validate our worth as human beings.

We typically desire success in order to validate our w_____ as human beings.

Our worth is based not on "success," but on having been created in the image of God. So, one of the greatest things to learn in life is that, by God's definition, success isn't necessary. Each of us has inherent and infinite worth because, and only because, we are created in the image of God. We have worth not because of what we accomplish, but because of who we are . . . we are His creation. God created us so that He could have a relationship with us, so He could be kind to us forever, so He could demonstrate to the world *through us* that He is who He says He is . . . omnipotent, omniscient, omnipresent, loving, just, kind, holy, and good.

If we insist on pursuing success as a measure of our worth, then two unpleasant things may happen.

First, circumstances may thwart us. We cannot control people, possessions, and circumstances well enough to guarantee success. Also, if we don't get what we want, we will be unsatisfied because we didn't get it. If we *do* get what we want, we will realize it does not satisfy. It is as Oscar Wilde famously said, "There are only two tragedies in life: one is not getting what one wants and the other is getting it." We climb the ladder of success only to find it was leaning against the wrong wall.

The second unpleasant thing that may happen to us is that God may pry our stubby little fingers, one at a time, off the thing we think will satisfy. He is the only thing (One) who can satisfy us completely and unendingly. And He loves us too much to allow us to go through life blindly trying to find satisfaction in anything other than Himself. He may induce failure so we will learn to transfer our affections to Him (Hebrews 12:5–11). John Newton (author of "Amazing Grace") once wrote, from God's perspective, "These earthly trials I employ from self and pride to set thee free, and break thy schemes of earthly joy that thou mayest seek thy all in Me."

4. True success is being faithful to God and leaving the results to Him.

True success is being f_____ to God and leaving the r_____ to Him.

In Joshua 1:8, God tells us what it takes to succeed in His eyes: "This Book of the Law shall not depart from your mouth, but you shall meditate on it day and night, so that you may be careful to do according to all that is written in it; for then you will make your way prosperous, and then you will achieve success."

We can see things a little more clearly if we think through the passage backward. For us to make our way prosperous and successful, we must do according to all that is written in the Book of the Law. In order to do all that is written in it, we must study and meditate on it continuously. *So, success comes when we are faithfully obedient to God's Word.* All we must do is discern as well as we can what God wants us to do and do it. That is success.

All the results belong to God. The apostle Paul wrote in 1 Corinthians 3:6: "I planted, Apollos watered, but God was causing the growth." This only reinforced the words of Jesus recorded by John: "Apart from Me you can do nothing" (John 15:5). We can bear no fruit without the Lord. Why? Because bearing fruit is beyond our ability. Only God can bring forth fruit. But He will use us to produce fruit through us if we are faithful to Him.

The single most discouraging person in the world to me when I first became a Christian was—surprisingly enough—Billy Graham. Don't get me wrong; I admired him more than I can say. It's just that I couldn't measure up to him. I felt hopelessly inferior.

I tried to be like Billy, and it soon became clear that this was not going to happen on any level. I concluded that he was going to get a fabulous mansion in heaven for his reward, but I was going to get a tar paper shack. In my spiritual infancy, I didn't realize one fundamental truth: God doesn't reward us on the basis of our results. He rewards us on the basis of our faithfulness to Him. He is the one who determines the results.

Conclusion

God may call a person like Billy Graham to a ministry that is very public, has a phenomenal response, and leads to worldwide recognition. Billy could have been 100% faithful to that call, or 50% faithful, or 0% faithful. And God will reward him *according to his faithfulness.*

On the other hand, God may call a person like our elderly friend to a very humble ministry of baking pies and sharing Jesus. And that person can be 100%, 50%, or 0% faithful. We all have an equal opportunity and ability to be *faithful to whatever God has called us.* Therefore, God can reward everyone equally.

God wants to bring us to the place where we realize that success doesn't satisfy and defeat doesn't destroy. The only thing that matters is whether we get up in the morning and say, "Lord, what do you want me to do today?" and whether we can lie down at night and say, "I did it." That is true success in God's eyes.

So, don't sink your own ship.
Trust God's definition of success.

CHAPTER REVIEW

Repetition is the key to mental ownership.

Success is being faithful to what God asks of us and leaving the results to Him.

1. Americans are preoccupied with s_____.
2. Success doesn't s_____.
3. We typically desire success in order to validate our w_____ as human beings.
4. True success is being f_____ to God and leaving the r_____ to Him.

 DON'T SINK YOUR OWN SHIP

If something is important, you must repeat it until it changes you.

Chapter Summaries

1. Look to God for h_____.
2. R_____ q_____ when you sin.
3. Be totally o_____ to God.
4. Be a good s_____ of life's resources.
5. Be a s_____ to others.
6. Choose the f_____ of self-discipline.
7. Don't let m_____ become m_____.
8. G_____ your mind to g_____ your life.
9. Use your tongue to h_____, not to h_____.
10. Trust God's definition of s_____.

 LIFE-CHECK

Answer these questions, either individually by journaling the answer or in a spiritual accountability group.

1. What is your greatest area of temptation for the world's success? In what ways do you get tricked into "walking after the carrot" of success?

2. Do you feel comfortable believing that God loves you simply because of who you are and not because of what you can accomplish? Think of someone you love. Do you love him or her because of what he or she has accomplished or because of who he or she is? Why is it difficult for Christians to relax in the confidence that God loves us unconditionally?

3. If we cannot produce spiritual results, should we be concerned? Why or why not?

 FOR FURTHER REFLECTION

Additional Scripture.

Joshua 1:8 1 Corinthians 3:6

Proverbs 27:20 Hebrews 12:5–11

John 15:5

 RESOURCES

For further study.

30 Days to Growing in Your Faith (Chapter 28), Max Anders

Success God's Way, Charles Stanley

CHAPTER 11

KEEP YOUR CONSCIENCE CLEAR

You must be willing to forgive and be forgiven, or your wounds will never heal and your conscience will never be clear.

Be kind to one another, compassionate, forgiving each other, just as God in Christ also has forgiven you.

—EPHESIANS 4:32

On April 27, 1990, Rusty sat on the edge of his narrow prison cell bunk on South Carolina's death row, his head and right leg shaved slick and moistened with conducting gel to help the two thousand volts of electricity enter his body and kill him for having committed brutal, senseless crimes.

Five years earlier, Rusty had sat comatose on the floor of his cell in such despair that when cockroaches crawled over his lap and shoulders, he didn't even bother to flick them off.

Prison Fellowship volunteer Bob McAlister, deputy chief of staff for the governor of South Carolina, sat down on the floor outside Rusty's cell and tried to talk to him. He did not respond.

He sat motionless, looking but not seeing, filthy, degraded, and utterly without hope. He had died already. But his heart had not stopped beating.

McAlister wrote:

Frustrated and scared, I prayed aloud that God would cut through the evil in that cell and pierce the heart of its inhabitant.

"Rusty, just say the word *Jesus*," I pleaded.

With much effort, he pursed his lips together and whispered, "Jesus."

"Just look at you," I gently chided. "Your cell's filthy and so are you. The roaches have taken over and you're spiritually a dead man, son. Jesus can give you something better."

I asked Rusty if he wanted to accept Jesus as Lord and Savior. Through tears, he nodded, then prayed. "Jesus, I've hurt a lot of people. Ain't no way that I deserve You to hear me. But I'm tired and I'm sick and I'm lonely. My mama's died and she's in heaven with You, and I never got to tell her bye. Please forgive me, Jesus, for everything I've done. I don't know much about You, but I'm willin' to learn, and I thank You for listenin' to me."

I went back to see him the next Monday. I walked up to his cell; it was spotless. Gone were the dirt and roaches and porno magazines. The walls were scrubbed, the bed was made, and the scent of disinfectant hung in the air.

"Bob, how do you like it?" exclaimed a smiling, energized Rusty. "I spent all weekend cleaning out my cell 'cause I figured that's what Jesus wanted me to do."

"Rusty," I blurted, "it took you all weekend to clean out your cell, but it took Jesus an instant to clean out your life."

Rusty and I became brothers in Christ. He loved to sit and listen as I read the Bible. During these quiet times of Bible reading, talking, and praying over four-and-a-half years, I hope I taught Rusty something about living. He taught me how to die.

As his appeals were turned down and his execution became a certainty, Rusty developed a simple vision of the hereafter: "When I get to heaven, Jesus and my mama are gonna be waitin' for me," he would say in his thick West Virginia drawl. "And my mama and me are gonna go fishin'."

[Hours before his execution], Rusty prayed, "Our precious Lord, I'm not crying 'cause I feel bad, but 'cause I'm happy. I'm gonna be with You, and You've done everything for me far beyond what I ever deserve. I ask You to watch over my family and take the hurt and sadness from their hearts. I pray that all of this pain and sufferin' will be gone and I just praise You with all of my heart."

The Holy Spirit was doing his final work in Rusty's life—and further work in mine. As we sat there the peace of God washed over us both—a peace that I cannot begin to describe. In that darkened, quiet cell after a frenetic day of emotional upheaval, God chose to move in our hearts, replacing their burdens and fears with the majestic assurance that Rusty would break away from the body of sin and suffering and be whisked away to heaven.

Rusty's body died at 1:05 a.m. that day, but I am convinced that he and his mama are fishin' in heavenly streams.[1]

Oh, my. What a story! What a dramatic example of the power of forgiveness! Before Rusty repented and accepted God's forgiveness, he had degenerated to the level of an animal, like a swine that doesn't bother to brush away the flies. But when he repented, was born again, and accepted the forgiveness Jesus offered him, he took off like a rocket on a steady, upward course of becoming like Christ.

It is difficult to overstate the power of forgiveness. Unless we are willing to forgive, our wounds will never heal. Unless we are willing to repent and be forgiven, our conscience will never be clear. In these simple facts lies one of the most profound truths of human existence, which is also one of the most commonly missed.

An unwillingness to repent and unwillingness to forgive, or an unwillingness or inability to accept forgiveness, has robbed the joy from as many lives as almost any other spiritual problem.

1. The Bible teaches that we must repent and seek forgiveness when we sin.

The Bible teaches that we must r_____ and seek f_____ when we sin.

God commands forgiveness because it's what we need. In Matthew 5:23–24 we read, "Therefore, if you are presenting your offering at the altar, and there you remember that your brother has something against you, leave your offering there before the altar and go; first be reconciled to your brother, and then come and present your offering."

It couldn't be much clearer. But repenting of sin is hard. Confessing it is harder. Asking for forgiveness is even harder. As a result, we rarely forgive. And our failure gets us into big trouble.

Many years ago when I was in seminary, there were two freight trains on the track of my life, rushing toward each other for a head-on collision. The first train was my study of the Hebrew language, the original language of the Old Testament. Hebrew is a difficult language to master. Rule number one in studying Hebrew? Never get behind! Period. If you do, you're done for. It takes all the time you have to keep up, and you cannot keep up and catch up at the same time.

I was getting behind. Why? The other freight train on my track was money. In addition to having trouble with Hebrew, I was also having trouble with money. In fact, I had too much Hebrew and not enough money! So, when I had the chance to work overtime near the end of a semester, I took it. I began working forty to forty-five hours a week just before final exams at the end of my second year. I knew it was a risk, but I didn't know what else to do.

I was able to keep up with all my classes except Hebrew. I got behind in that class and couldn't catch up.

The course rule was this: No matter what your daily grades and other exam scores were, you had to pass the final exam or you could not pass the course. And you had to pass the course to graduate from seminary. Hebrew was offered only once a year, so if I failed this course, I would have to stay in seminary another year just to make up that one course. That was unthinkable. I couldn't afford it financially or emotionally. To say the least, a lot was riding on this final exam, and I doubted if I could pass it.

When the fateful day came, the instructors herded all the sections of second-year Hebrew into one small room to take the test at the same time. The room was too small. The chairs were the old wooden kind with a right-armed desktop. To get us all in, the instructors had to push the chairs so close together that they nearly touched.

Did you know that if you cup your hand on your forehead just above your eyes, you can look through the cracks in your fingers and see perfectly clearly, although no one can see where you're looking? You appear to be concentrating diligently on the paper on your desk, but you can see the papers on both sides of you if you switch hands. The guy on my left was a whiz kid. He was translating the Hebrew with little more effort than it would take me to read Dr. Seuss.

I wrote what he wrote, and then I doublechecked his accuracy with the guy on my right, who was no slouch either. I even slipped in a few deliberate mistakes of my own, so my paper wouldn't be exactly like anyone else's. I wasn't greedy. I didn't need an A—all I needed was a C.

I thought I was saved. I would pass the course and graduate from seminary.

Surprisingly, my cheating brought only minor twinges of conscience because I felt my personal circumstances had backed me into an impossible corner. I figured it was easier to get forgiveness than permission. So I cheated, told the Lord I was sorry, and went on with my life.

Several months later I had the profound misfortune of attending a seminar in which the leader talked about cleansing your conscience and how a clear conscience is the basis of all moral authority. I had been to this seminar several times before and knew that he always spoke about this, but I had forgotten. If I had remembered, I never would have attended.

When the teacher got to the "cleansed conscience" part, I began to get uncomfortable. My discomfort resembled the feeling you have when you remember you are going to the dentist. I began to fidget. My heartbeat sped up. My breathing elevated slightly. The Holy Spirit was putting me in a great spiritual vice and cranking down the pressure: "If you want to be like Jesus, you cannot cheat your way out of problems! Pastors' lives are not built on dishonesty! You have sinned against God, violated the standards of the school, and damaged your own moral authority!"

I was in big trouble, and I knew it. Again, I was faced with two impossible choices: Either I could spit in the face of God and reject His work in my heart, or I could go back to my Hebrew professor and confess to him that I had cheated. I felt a little of what David wrote about in Psalm 32 after one of his great sins:

> When I kept silent about my sin, my body wasted away
> Through my groaning all day long.
> For day and night Your hand was heavy upon me;
> My vitality failed as with the dry heat of summer.
>
> (vv. 3–4)

After an eternity of wrestling with God, pleading with Him to let me off the hook, promising that I would never do it again, and having God stonewall me, I finally broke. I confessed my sin on a deep level, acknowledged my lack of trust in Him, asked for forgiveness, and agreed with God to make it right.

I made an appointment with my Hebrew professor to tell him what I had done. I didn't know what would happen. At the least, I would fail the class, have to stay in school another year to make it up, and graduate a year late. At worst, I could be kicked out of seminary. Maybe my transgression would go on my transcript, and whenever I tried to get a job in a church, a letter from the seminary would say, "Overall, he was a decent student, but the little stinker will cheat if you let him." Maybe they would stamp that sentence on my forehead.

When I finished my story, the professor (may his tribe increase!) said, "Well, Max, I think you have learned a lesson more important than Hebrew. I'll make a deal with you. Since there were extenuating circumstances, I will give you an incomplete for this course, and if you take the next required Hebrew course and pass it, I will give you a 'C' for this course. How is that?"

My first impulse was to clutch his ankles and weep quietly on his shoe tops. Instead, I merely said, "That would be fine. Thank you." And I walked out of his office.

I felt deeply cleansed. Pure. Holy. I wanted to laugh and cry at the same time. I wanted to run and jump and dance. The burden was lifted. The chains were broken. I was free!

I was so deeply grateful to God, not because the worst hadn't happened—I was prepared for that. I was filled with joy because I felt forgiven. God would not let me sweep my sin under the rug where it would rot like old cheese. He loved me enough to make me go through the pain of correcting it Jesus's way. Now, no one could ever say to me, "You cheated, and you never made it right."

If we don't ask for forgiveness when we wrong someone, we lose our moral authority; the debris of sin begins to accumulate in our hearts, choking our consciences, and we lose our reputation as people of integrity. Others know when we sin against them, and if we don't make it right, it hurts our reputation as well as God's.

Forgiveness is a two-edged sword. We have only put our thumb to one edge so far—namely, that we must repent and seek forgiveness when we sin. We look now at the second edge.

2. The Bible teaches that we must be willing to forgive others when they sin against us.

The Bible teaches that we must be willing to f_____ others when they sin against us.

In Matthew 18:21–22, Peter asked Jesus how many times he ought to forgive the brother who sins against him. "Up to seven times?" he asked, probably thinking he had really gone the extra mile. Jesus responded, "I do not say to you, up to seven times, but up to seventy-seven times."

Additionally, when Jesus taught His disciples to pray in the Lord's Prayer, He included, "And forgive us our debts, as we also have forgiven our debtors" (Matthew 6:12).

The hurt others inflict on us and the resentment this generates is one of the hardest things in the Christian life to get over. You may want revenge—an eye for an eye—or worse. You may want to vindicate yourself. You may want to let the world see that it was the other person and not you who was wrong. There are countless ways we can be hurt and an equal number of forms our bitterness and resentment can take.

Our bitterness and resentment bubbles, boils, and stews in our hearts until the unholy mess fills our lives with a stench. Then we eat the mess over days, weeks, months, or years. The chief drawback is that we are consuming ourselves. The carcass after the meal is us. Often the other person(s) know nothing about our hurt, or if they do, they have effortlessly ignored it. We are the ones who suffer.

The pain dominates our lives. It disrupts other relationships (Hebrews 12:14–15). It costs us sleep, peace, and normal living.

There is only one way to stop this self-inflicted carnage—we must forgive. That's not to say that we shouldn't take steps to correct a wrong, but whatever action we take, we must first forgive. This is, as I said, one of the hardest things in the Christian life to do, but it is one of the most necessary.

Forgiveness is often an act of the will followed by a process. Like a trick candle that starts burning again after it is blown out, or like Frankenstein's monster, resentment comes back to life again. That doesn't mean we didn't forgive in the first place. It just means that whenever we are tempted to take up the offense again, we must forgive again—or remind ourselves that we have already forgiven and are not going to take up the offense again.

3. Forgiveness is essential to spiritual freedom.

Forgiveness is essential to spiritual f_____.

This principle is one of the most important in the Christian life. Without it we are a slave to our past. With it we are free in Christ.

Forgiveness is so hard, yet so necessary. It is necessary for us to seek forgiveness from those we have wronged, or we will never have a clear conscience. It is necessary for us to forgive those who hurt us, or our wounds and relationships will never heal.

Forgiveness is an act of the will, and we can forgive regardless of the inclination of our heart.

Put yourself in this true story. Corrie ten Boom was a Dutch Christian who was sent to a concentration camp in Germany during World War II for harboring escaping Jews. She endured almost unspeakable suffering at the hands of the Nazis, but survived and began a speaking ministry after the war.

Corrie eventually faced a dramatic challenge to her willingness to forgive. She was speaking in Germany, bringing her audience the message that God forgives. After she finished speaking, and as people were leaving the crowded room, Corrie saw a man who was a guard in the Nazi concentration camp where she had been imprisoned. She wrote of her experience in her book *Tramp for the Lord*:

> I saw him, working his way forward against the others. One moment I saw the overcoat and the brown hat; the next, a blue uniform and a visored cap with its skull and crossbones. It came back with a rush: the huge room with its harsh overhead lights; the pathetic pile of dresses and shoes in the center of the floor; the shame of walking naked past this man. I could see my sister's frail form ahead of me, ribs sharp beneath the parchment skin. . . .
>
> The place was Ravensbruck and the man who was making his way forward had been a guard—one of the most cruel guards.
>
> Now he was in front of me, hand thrust out: "A fine message, Fraulein! How good it is to know that, as you say, all our sins are at the bottom of the sea!"
>
> And I, who had spoken so glibly of forgiveness, fumbled in my pocketbook rather than take that hand. He would not remember me, of course—how could he remember one prisoner among those thousands of women?
>
> But I remembered him and the leather crop swinging from his belt. I was face-to-face with one of my captors and my blood seemed to freeze.
>
> "You mentioned Ravensbruck in your talk," he was saying. "I was a guard there." No, he did not remember me.
>
> "But since that time . . . I have become a Christian. I know that God has forgiven me for the cruel things I did there, but I would like to hear it from your lips as well. Fraulein,"—again the hand came out—"will you forgive me?"
>
> And I stood there—I whose sins had again and again to be forgiven—and could not forgive. Betsie [my sister] had died

in that place—could he erase her slow terrible death simply for the asking?

It could not have been many seconds that he stood there—hand held out—but to me it seemed hours as I wrestled with the most difficult thing I had ever had to do. . . .

The coldness [was] clutching my heart. But forgiveness is not an emotion—I knew that too. Forgiveness is an act of the will, and the will can function regardless of the temperature of the heart. "Jesus, help me!" I prayed silently. "I can lift my hand. I can do that much. You supply the feeling."

And so woodenly, mechanically, I thrust my hand into the one stretched out to me. And as I did, an incredible thing took place. The current started in my shoulder, raced down my arm, sprang into our joined hands. And then this healing warmth seemed to flood my whole being, bringing tears to my eyes.

"I forgive you, brother!" I cried. "With all my heart."

For a long moment we grasped each other's hands, the former guard and the former prisoner.[2]

Does someone come to mind who has hurt you? Have you forgiven him or her? If not, do so now. Does someone come to mind whom you have wronged? Pray and ask the Lord what you should do to correct it.

So, don't sink your own ship.
Keep your conscience clear.

CHAPTER REVIEW

Repetition is the key to mental ownership.

You must be willing to forgive and be forgiven, or your wounds will never heal and your conscience will never be clear.

1. The Bible teaches that we must r_____ and seek f_____ when we sin.
2. The Bible teaches that we must be willing to f_____ others when they sin against us.
3. Forgiveness is essential to spiritual f_____.

DON'T SINK YOUR OWN SHIP

If something is important, you must repeat it until it changes you.

Chapter Summaries

1. Look to God for h_____.
2. R_____ q_____ when you sin.
3. Be totally o_____ to God.
4. Be a good s_____ of life's resources.
5. Be a s_____ to others.
6. Choose the f_____ of self-discipline.
7. Don't let m_____ become m_____.
8. G_____ your mind to g_____ your life.
9. Use your tongue to h_____, not to h_____.
10. Trust God's definition of s_____.
11. Keep your c_____ clear.

LIFE-CHECK

Answer these questions, either individually by journaling the answer or in a spiritual accountability group.

1. Are you struggling with hurt and/or resentment over something someone did to you? Have you forgiven him or her or them? If not, is there any reason you could not forgive now?
2. Have you forgiven someone who's hurt you but find the feelings of anger and resentment returning (Hebrews 12:15)? Did you realize that forgiveness can be a process after the initial act? Is there any reason why, if you need to, you could not forgive again, or perhaps remind yourself that you have already forgiven, so that you are not manipulated by your emotions?
3. Is there anyone you need to ask for forgiveness? Is there any reason why you could not determine to ask that person to forgive you as soon as it is practical? Is there any restitution you need to offer?
4. Do you feel the lack of moral authority associated with a conscience that isn't clear? Would you like to experience the freedom and joy of a clear conscience? Are you willing to make the sacrifice to obtain this?

 FOR FURTHER REFLECTION

Additional Scripture.

Psalm 32:3–4	2 Corinthians 2:3–11
Matthew 5:23–24	Ephesians 4:29–32
Matthew 6:9–13	Hebrews 12:15
Matthew 18:15–35	

 RESOURCES

For further study.

30 Days to Growing in Your Faith (Chapter 16), Max Anders

The Scandal of Forgiveness, Philip Yancey

CHAPTER 12

NURTURE YOUR RELATIONSHIPS

DON'T SINK YOUR OWN SHIP.
NURTURE YOUR RELATIONSHIPS.

It is people, not things, that make life worthwhile.

Greater love has no one than this, that a person will lay down
his life for his friends.

—JOHN 15:13

When you strip everything away, life really comes down to this:
knowing we are not alone, knowing somebody cares, and
knowing we are loved.

Early in his administration, President Ronald Reagan came out
of the Hilton hotel where he had just spoken and was walking a
short distance to his car when he heard a noise—*pop, pop, pop*—like
firecrackers going off. His Secret Service bodyguard shoved him
into the nearby presidential limousine and jumped in on top of
him. Reagan felt a crushing pain in his ribs and thought that his
bodyguard had broken one of the ribs. Only later did Reagan learn
that the pain was from a gunshot wound.

Reagan began coughing up blood, and the Secret Service rushed him to George Washington Hospital. He was able to start walking to the emergency room, but then got lightheaded and weak in the knees. He was also having great difficulty breathing. The next thing Reagan knew, he was lying face up on a gurney, being wheeled into the hospital. Later, as he was going into the operating room, he looked at the surgical team and quipped, "I sure hope you're all Republicans."

However, President Reagan's breathing difficulties had increased earlier while he was still in the emergency room. His lungs were working, but no matter how many times he took a breath, he couldn't get enough air, even though the ER staff had an oxygen tube down his throat. He began to panic and finally blacked out.

When Reagan regained consciousness some time later, he felt someone, evidently one of the nurses, holding his hand. He later wrote, "It is difficult for me to describe how deeply touched I was by that gesture. It was very reassuring just to feel the warmth of a human hand."

He was still not fully conscious and could not see who was holding his hand, giving him such a surge of encouragement. "Who's holding my hand?" he asked. There was no answer. "Who's holding my hand?" he asked again. Again, no answer. "Does Nancy know about us?"[1]

For the most powerful man on earth, the most important thing to him at that desperate moment was to feel the warmth of a caring hand.

"We are all born for love. It is the principle of existence and its only end." So said Benjamin Disraeli, former prime minister of the United Kingdom.

This captures the essence of how God has created us—to love and be loved. In John 15:12, Jesus said, "This is My commandment, that you love one another, just as I have loved you."

Harold Kushner, in his book *When All You Ever Wanted Isn't Enough*, wrote:

> I was sitting on a beach one summer day, watching two children, a boy and a girl, playing in the sand. They were hard at work building an elaborate sand castle by the water's edge, with gates and towers and moats and internal passages. Just when they had nearly finished their project, a big wave came along and knocked it down, reducing it to a heap of wet sand. I expected the children to burst into tears, devastated by what had happened to all their hard work. But they surprised me. Instead, they ran up the shore away from the water, laughing and holding hands, and sat down to build another castle. I realized that they had taught me an important lesson. All the things in our lives, all the complicated structures we spend so much time and energy creating, are built on sand. Only our relationships to other people endure. Sooner or later, the wave will come along and knock down what we have worked so hard to build up. When that happens, only the person who has somebody's hand to hold will be able to laugh.[2]

God has created us to live in harmony and unity with other humans, and unless we have meaningful relationships, life becomes hard.

Billy Graham often said that the number one most popular sermon he preached was on loneliness. In our look-out-for-number-one culture, we have gotten what we looked out for: ourselves. And we find that *we* are not enough. We feel alienated, isolated, and lonely.

Our culture is highly mobile, self-centered, and pleasure-driven. As a result, we may never get rooted—we may never get a sense of belonging—we may never rid ourselves of loneliness. Why? Because it is not the self-centered accumulation of things or the struggle to succeed that gives joy and meaning to life, but, rather, people are what make life worth living.

1. The fundamental principle governing life's key relationships is to respect one another.

The fundamental principle governing life's key relationships is to r_____ one another.

In Ephesians 5:22–6:9, the apostle Paul discusses three sets of relationships: husband/wife, parent/child, and employer/employee. Husbands are instructed to love their wives as Christ loved the church and gave Himself for her. Wives are to respect their husbands. Parents are to bring their children up in the training and admonition of the Lord. Children are to obey their parents. Employers (masters) are to treat their employees (servants) well, knowing that their own master is in heaven. Employees are to obey their employer and serve him or her as they would Christ.

In each of these relationships there are common principles. First, someone is in authority and someone is in submission. Second, the one in authority is to serve the one in submission. Third, the one in submission is to respect the authority of the one in authority.

The primary responsibility for nurturing key relationships lies on the shoulders of the one in authority—the husband, the parents, and the employer. Certainly it takes two to tango, and an unresponsive wife, child, or employee can thwart the sincerest of efforts. But that doesn't change the principle.

The bottom line is that we must respect each other and treat one another with appropriate respect. If someone doesn't respect us, we instinctively sense this, and it interferes with a satisfying relationship.

The husband is to love his wife as Christ loved the church and gave Himself up for her, while the wife is to respect her husband.

I have seen heartbreaking disintegration of marriages because one or both parties in the marriage failed to nurture the relationship.

Sometimes it was out of ignorance. Other times it was out of misplaced priorities (jobs, hobbies, money, other people), laziness, or wrong ideas.

I have had husbands tell me that their wives left them. It was a bombshell—the husband had no warning. After much conversation, however, in too many cases I'd learn that the husband wooed and nurtured his wife until they were married. Then, that job done, he went on to other things. The wife felt neglected, unappreciated, and unloved. After a while she decided it wasn't worth it. If the husband had spent anywhere near the same time and energy nurturing the relationship *after* marriage as he did *before*, the breakup might never have happened.

That in no way condones leaving a spouse for unbiblical reasons. It does mean, however, that if you want your marriage to grow, whether you are a husband or a wife, you have to nurture it.

The parents are to rear their children in the nurture and admonition of the Lord, while the children are to obey their parents.

Heartbreak among parents over the lives of their children has become epidemic. Too many times the children of well-meaning parents go off the deep end and shipwreck or at least seriously damage their lives, and this might have been avoided.

Some problems include:

- *Absentee fathers.* The mother is not necessarily a single parent. The father may be living in the same house, but he is not significantly involved in the life of his child.
- *Being more concerned with external "things" than relationships.* A preoccupation with material comfort, looking good to others, or structure and discipline over relationships can seriously weaken the bond with children.
- *Inadequate or undemonstrated love between parents.* It is often said that the greatest gift parents can give their children is a

home where the love between the husband and wife is secure and obvious.

Imagine a lifeguard sitting in his chair enjoying the delightful weather, when suddenly a swimmer needs help. The lifeguard shouldn't consider that an interruption; the swimmers are his primary responsibility. Similarly, parents need to sit on a high chair in life, looking out over the beach of life for their children and making sure everything is okay with them. If the children need something, this should not be considered an interruption.

Whenever parents place any priority in life higher than their child (except for their relationship with the Lord or their spouse), the child instinctively understands and looks someplace else for security and significance. This "elsewhere" is typically the child's peers. If this happens, the child begins to adopt the value system of his or her peers, which, if it doesn't include close family ties, can often result in rapid deterioration of the relationships within the family.

The employer is to treat his employees with proper respect and fairness, while the employees are to serve their employer ethically.

Ephesians 6:5–9 teaches us that we must do our jobs as though we were working for Christ Himself. Whether we are in labor or management, whether we are an employee or employer, it doesn't matter.

If you are an employer or in management, and you want a better relationship with your workers, putting this principle in action will do two things for you: (1) It will give you happier workers, a more stable workforce, and a more productive workforce; and (2) it will, in the end, be better for your profit/loss statement. But you must work at this. You must find out what the needs of your employees are and do your best to meet those needs, both physical and emotional.

While finances are always important to workers, there is another thing that, in some studies, has proven to be equally important: R-E-S-P-E-C-T! Workers want to know they are valued, appreciated, and respected. Good relationships with employees will happen only if those relationships are nurtured by those in authority.

On the other hand, there are things employees can also do to nurture relationships. First, they can respect and honor their employers, working for them as they would Christ. Of course, this means that you don't do illegal or unethical things, and you must do the work responsibly.

In addition, you must nurture your relationships with coworkers. This is often a significant challenge since some coworkers can be disagreeable. However, Jesus would treat others with respect if He were in our shoes, and, therefore, so must we.

I remember hearing the story of a tollbooth attendant who was known for her friendliness and efficiency. When asked what her secret was to finding happiness in such a boring job, she replied that shortly after she began working there, she realized that if she looked at her job merely as handing out change to people, she would soon go crazy. So she envisioned her job as trying to turn her brief encounters with drivers into opportunities to make their lives a little happier. The money became incidental. She found happiness in her job by serving a higher purpose than her specific function. That is what the Lord wants us all to do in the workplace.

2. In order to have friends, you must be a friend.

In order to h_____ friends, you must b__ a friend.

The Bible does not speak about friendships as systematically as it does husbands/wives, parents/children, and employers/employees, but it does shed light on this subject.

Friendship was highly valued by Jesus.

- Jesus said, regarding his disciples, "No longer do I call you slaves . . . I have called you friends (John 15:15).
- Again, Jesus said, "Greater love has no one than this, that a person will lay down his life for his friends" (John 15:13).
- Finally, Jesus said, "By this all people will know that you are My disciples: if you have love for one another" (John 13:35).

Beyond Jesus's teaching, Scripture speaks generally to principles of friendship.

- "A friend loves at all times, and a brother is born for adversity" (Proverbs 17:17).
- "As iron sharpens iron, so one person sharpens another" (Proverbs 27:17).
- "Do not make friends with a person given to anger" (Proverbs 22:24).
- "Two are better than one because they have a good return for their labor; for if either of them falls, the one will lift up his companion" (Ecclesiastes 4:9–10).
- "Do not be deceived: 'Bad company corrupts good morals'" (1 Corinthians 15:33).

There are any number of ways we can be a friend . . . to

- Respect
- Honor
- Affirm
- Listen
- Counsel
- Serve
- Trust
- Etc.

Beyond all this, others have made powerful observations about friendship:

To the ancients, friendship seemed the happiest and most fully human of all loves; the crown of life in the school of virtue. The modern world, in comparison, ignores it. —*C. S. Lewis*

Friendship is the greatest of worldly goods. Certainly to me it is the chief happiness of life. If I had to give a piece of advice to a young [person] about a place to live, I think I should say, "Sacrifice almost everything to live where you can be near your friends." —*C. S. Lewis*

Two things are essential in this world—life, and friendship. Both must be highly prized, and not undervalued.
—*St. Augustine*

Friendship is the highest happiness of all moral agents.
—*Jonathan Edwards*

I think to a feeling mind there is no temporal pleasure equal to the pleasure of friendship. —*John Newton*

Conclusion

Being from the rich farm country of northern Indiana, I love the soil. When I was growing up, the soil where we lived—to my child's eyes—seemed to be so rich that when our family wanted a garden, all we had to do was dig up the soil and throw the seeds out on the ground! The next morning we would come out, and the garden would be up and growing. Two days later we would be picking tomatoes and pulling carrots. We grew ears of corn so large that our family of eight could all eat off of one ear at the same time (or so it seemed at that time).

After I graduated from seminary in Dallas, my wife Margie and I lived the early years of our marriage in Phoenix, Portland, and then Atlanta. In Phoenix it was too hot and dry to grow a good garden. In Portland it was too cold and wet. When we got to Atlanta, I was determined to have a garden. The soil in Atlanta is red clay and very acidic, so I talked to some people who knew about soil preparation. Following their advice, I tilled into the ground a pile of compost half the size of Pikes Peak. Then, to neutralize the acid in the soil, I tilled in enough lime to dust the state of Rhode Island. Finally, I planted the corn, beans, tomatoes, and zucchini and sat back to wait for harvest day.

As the beans came up, the rabbits held a convention in our backyard and served our bean sprouts for the main course one night. We never again saw any evidence of having planted beans. Then the raccoons plucked the corn the instant it developed any moisture in the kernels. The tomato plants grew gloriously to about two feet high, developed a profusion of brilliant yellow flowers . . . and fell over dead. Cutworms. We got some powder to get rid of the cutworms, and the two remaining plants began to develop actual tomatoes. They grew to about the size of a peach, turned a delightful light pink, split open, and died. There was still too much acid in the soil. We never ate a tomato from that garden.

The only vegetable we were able to harvest was zucchini—ten of them. I don't even *like* zucchini, but I was able to *grow* it. We had bad luck with rabbits, raccoons, and cutworms. But we were onto the right idea. We just gave up too soon. Having a good garden can be a lot of work, and there were people in Atlanta who had put in the work and reaped the reward.

We spent about one hundred twenty dollars on the garden—composting, tilling, adding lime, more tilling, planting seeds and seedlings, watering, etc. That figured out to about twelve dollars a zucchini. You can buy a zucchini for less—a lot less. In fact, I learned that if you know someone with a good garden, this person can grow zucchini too, and will give you more than you'd ever want even if you *like* it. (In a lifestyle magazine, I read the warning: "Danger! Keep your car doors locked! It's zucchini season!")

This episode ended my gardening career for decades, until I learned more about how to *nurture* a garden along. But it struck me how similar cultivating friendships is to cultivating a garden. American poet Henry W. Longfellow said it well:

> Kind hearts are the garden,
> Kind thoughts are the roots,
> Kind words are the flowers,
> Kind deeds are the fruits.
> Take care of your garden
> And keep out the weeds,
> Fill it with sunshine,
> Kind words, and kind deeds.

If you blow it with your garden, you just end up with twelve-dollar zucchinis and a good story to tell. But if you blow it with your spouse or your kids or your friends, the price can be devastating.

Tend your relationships with love . . . giving to them. In God's design, relationships will only *grow* as you *nurture* them.

So, DON'T SINK YOUR OWN SHIP.
NURTURE YOUR RELATIONSHIPS.

CHAPTER REVIEW

Repetition is the key to mental ownership.

It is people, not things, that make life worthwhile.

1. The fundamental principle governing life's key relationships is to r_____ one another.
2. In order to h_____ friends, you must b__ a friend.

 DON'T SINK YOUR OWN SHIP

If something is important, you must repeat it until it changes you.

Chapter Summaries

1. Look to God for h_____.
2. R_____ q_____ when you sin.
3. Be totally o_____ to God.
4. Be a good s_____ of life's resources.
5. Be a s_____ to others.
6. Choose the f_____ of self-discipline.
7. Don't let m_____ become m_____.
8. G_____ your mind to g_____ your life.
9. Use your tongue to h_____, not to h_____.
10. Trust God's definition of s_____.
11. Keep your c_____ clear.
12. Nurture your r_____.

 LIFE-CHECK

Answer these questions, either individually by journaling the answer or in a spiritual accountability group.

1. Do you have enough friends, or are you lonely, alienated, and rootless? If you do not have enough meaningful relationships, why do you think this is happening?
2. In the past, what significance have you given to friendships? What significance do you think you will give the matter in future decisions?
3. Do you have good friendships in your family? Why or why not? What are ways you might improve your relationships within your family? How about within your church?

 FOR FURTHER REFLECTION

Additional Scripture.
> Proverbs 18:24
> Proverbs 27:10
> John 15:13–15

RESOURCES

For further study.
> *Love and Respect*, Emerson Eggerichs (Husband/wife relationships)
> *How to Really Love Your Child*, Ross Campbell (Parent/child relationships)
> *Every Good Endeavor*, Timothy Keller (Employer/employee relationships)
> *Made for Friendship*, Drew Hunter
> *Friendish*, Kelly Needham

CHAPTER 13

PAY THE PRICE TO BE PATIENT

Don't sink your own ship.
Pay the price to be patient.

You must be willing to give up a dime today to gain a dollar tomorrow.

If you have been raised with Christ, keep seeking the things that are above, where Christ is, seated at the right hand of God. Set your minds on the things that are above, not on the things that are on earth.

—COLOSSIANS 3:1-2

A snail was oozing its way across the garden when a turtle came up and mugged him. When the garden police got there, they asked the snail if he could give them a description of the turtle. The snail said, "No—it all happened so fast!"

In contrast to this, there are things in life that happen to us very slowly. These things require patience, and we don't like moving slowly. We want things to speed up so we can be rid of them. Most of us don't want to be patient.

I remember when I was very young, perhaps four or five years old, and had just eaten a peach. One of my siblings told me that the seed on the inside was what peach trees grew from. They told me that if I planted the seed, a peach tree would grow from it and bear more peaches.

Eager to witness this phenomenon, I scurried to the backyard where I planted the peach seed in the sandbox. I slept that night with visions of peach trees dancing in my head. The next morning, I went out to the sandbox. There was no peach tree. As I stood there, the disappointment grew rapidly to anger. I ripped the peach seed out of the sandbox and threw it as far as my chubby little fingers could throw it into the field adjoining our backyard.

I have been struggling for patience ever since.

1. Patience is a virtue.

Patience is a v_____.

While individuals in our culture often struggle with patience, our better cultural influences recognize patience as a virtue.

To lose patience is to lose the battle.

—*Mahatma Gandhi*

He that can have patience can have what he will.

—*Benjamin Franklin*

The strongest of all warriors are these two: time and patience.

—*Leo Tolstoy*

Beyond this, the Bible views patience as a virtue:
- Patience is a fruit of the Spirit (Galatians 5:22–23).
- Patience is a mark of biblical love (1 Corinthians 13:4).
- Patience is a virtue that Jesus modeled for our benefit (1 Timothy 1:16).

I think patience is such a difficult virtue because you don't *do* anything. With the virtue of diligence, you do something. With the virtue of honesty, you do something. But with patience, you don't do anything. You just wait. Most of us don't wait well.

2. Patience is required for life irritations.

Patience is required for life i_____.

Irritations come at us almost continuously as we live everyday life. We all identify with the prayer, "Lord, give me patience . . . and hurry!"

We might need patience for relentless bad traffic, for the questions of a toddler, or the irritations of a careless and obnoxious coworker.

I do not intend to imply that these things are "nothing." If we do not cope with them, we can all die the death of a thousand small cuts. But they are certainly easier to deal with than truly life-altering things that require patience—or else!

For the normal irritations of life, I have found the following "patience hacks" personally invaluable.

Patience Hack #1: Serve the Lord by serving the offenders.

Years ago, my wife and I lived in Atlanta—a rapidly growing city that has never been able to catch up to its need for more highways. It is a large and sprawling city, and on good days I had to drive forty-five minutes each way from home to work. On bad days (meaning on days when there were accidents) it could easily go to sixty to seventy-five minutes each way. It was not unheard of to spend an hour and a half on the road each day— sometimes more.

That kind of traffic can do a number on your brain. You can get very possessive about your spot in the line, very jealous about cars not taking turns, and very resentful of rude drivers.

I would often end up at my office in a boiling rage, and I then had to sit down and write about how people should live a good Christian life.

There's something wrong with this picture, I thought.

So, I determined that I would serve the Lord by serving other drivers. I determined to be courteous to other drivers who were careless, I determined to be generous to other drivers who were stingy, and I determined to be cautious of other drivers who were reckless. I determined to try to help make the world a little better by how I drove. I even thought to myself, *This might catch on and I might be able to initiate a highway revival in Atlanta.*

If you have been through Atlanta lately, you know that I did not initiate a highway revival, but my new mindset initiated my own revival and changed my life in a significant way.

Some years later, I was further instructed and affirmed in my decision to serve the Lord by serving those who irritate me when I heard a child saying to her mother who was taking her to childcare, "Mommy, I don't think God wants you to talk to the other drivers like that."

Patience Hack #2: Visualize the forthcoming experience.

The brain does not distinguish between a real and a vividly imagined event. That is why athletes spend significant amounts of time visualizing peak athletic performance. That is what golfers are doing when they step up to the tee and stare down the fairway before taking their swing. They are visualizing the perfect golf shot, which research proves will help them be more successful.

If I know that I will be going into a situation that requires patience, I find it helpful to visualize myself being in the situation and responding appropriately before the event gets there. *Rehearsing* appropriate behavior *helps produce* appropriate behavior. And, remember that "*Repetition is the key to mental ownership!*" This leads us to Patience Hack #3.

Patience Hack #3: Rehearse Scripture and/or affirmations about patience regularly.

It can be very helpful to rehearse Scripture or affirmations on a daily basis, even if you aren't aware of an upcoming situation in which you will need patience.

This does three things:

1. It allows the Holy Spirit to convict you of sin and call you to righteousness (John 16:8).
2. It allows the brain to rewire itself, physically improving your ability to act consistently with the scriptural truth, preparing you ahead of time for irritations that might otherwise have caused you to respond impatiently.
3. It kicks in the reticular activating system, that cerebral doorkeeper which allows things into your brain. When your brain sees that acting patiently is a value to you, you will be able to see things in your environment that support this value. You would likely have missed these things if you weren't rehearsing that truth.

One of my affirmations is, "I leave behind small attitudes, values, and behaviors, and I rise to great ones." I'm not perfect in executing this, but I do much better than if I didn't rehearse.

Patience Hack #4: Determine not to be manipulated by the enemy.

The enemy plays mind games with Christians. For example, in Ephesians 4:26–27 we see that if we do not readily repent of anger, the devil is given a spiritual warfare advantage in our life.

If Satan knows that you will not resist a temptation toward impatience, he will dangle a situation in front of you, like a matador dangling a cape before a bull, knowing that it cannot resist charging the cape. Being aware that the devil was manipulating me like this was a powerful motivation for me. I would look at a situation that might normally elicit a strong reaction of impatience, and then something would click in my mind, saying, "I am not going to let Satan manipulate me like that." This gave me valuable patience.

Patience Hack #5: Give grace and choose to behave better than difficult people around you.

We cannot know what experiences difficult people might have had as children growing up. They might be scarred by things that might have scarred us, too, if we'd had the same experience.

Who knows what kind of person I might be if I had had the same experiences others have had? So, it was helpful for me to have a measure of understanding like that, and then to determine that I was not going to respond to others in like fashion.

Benjamin Franklin wrote, "Doing an injury puts you below your enemy. Revenging one makes you but even with him. Forgiving it sets you above him." It's not Scripture—but it's still true. The only way we can be greater than those who offend us is to be patient with them.

So, to grow in our ability to cope patiently with normal *everyday life irritations*, we can try these five helpful "hacks" for increasing our patience.

3. Patience is required for the hard experiences of life.

Patience is required for the h_____ experiences of life.

We used to joke with our daughter when she was growing up that she should not become a doctor because she would never have any patients (patience). The reality is, many of us could use the same caution. All agree that patience is a virtue, but few excel in it. (By the way, now a loving wife and mother, our daughter is teaching the virtue of patience to her own young daughter.)

To be patient in the big, hard things of life requires an eternal perspective. "Big things" that require patience are a form of "trial," and trials can only be dealt with by viewing them as God does.

Without an eternal perspective, we are playing checkers in life while God is playing chess.

We make all the wrong moves and lose in the end.

All human beings are also, and foremost, spiritual beings—the part of us that lives forever. As Christians, we need to also understand that we are no longer citizens of this world. We are now citizens of another world. Philippians 3:20 says, "For our citizenship is in heaven, from which we also eagerly wait for a Savior, the Lord Jesus Christ." Also, Colossians 1:13 says, "For He rescued us from the domain of darkness, and transferred us to the kingdom of His beloved Son . . ."

It is just as the old "spiritual song" sings:

> This world is not my home, I'm just passing through.
> If heaven's not my home, then Lord, what will I do?
> The angels beckon me from heaven's open door,
> And I can't feel at home in this world anymore.

As citizens of another world, we have different values, priorities, and expectations.

Perhaps you've heard the story about the missionary couple years ago returning to the United States on a passenger ship, after having spent a lifetime in service to the Lord in central Africa.

Coincidentally, Teddy Roosevelt was returning home on the same ship after one of his famous hunting safaris in Africa. When the ship pulled up to dock, bands were playing, flags were waving, and dignitaries were lined up to meet him. Major league hoopla and whoop-de-do greeted the returning president.

The missionary husband leaned on the railing watching the celebration, and said to his wife, "The president goes on a hunting trip, and the world turns out to meet him when he returns. We spend our entire lives serving the Lord in Africa, and when we come home there isn't even anyone to meet us."

After a brief silence his wife replied, "But the difference is, we are not home yet."

And, that *is* the difference. They weren't home yet. When Christians do get home, the heavenly bands will play, celestial confetti will fly, and saintly dignitaries will be on hand. There'll be a parade in paradise down the streets of gold. Until then, life is likely to treat us worse than a Yankee manager in a Dodger dugout.

Does life seem all uphill to you? You're not home yet. Do life's rewards seem to pass you by? You're not home yet. Do you have longings that are not fulfilled by anything on earth? You're not home yet. Don't expect this world to treat you as though you were actually home.

This world isn't our home; we're just passing through. Be patient. Be willing to wait until you get home to receive your reward. Live for your citizenship in heaven. An eternal perspective is the key to cultivating patience in the face of life's hard times.

4. Patience is developed through trials.

Patience is developed through t_____.

Patience does not come easily or passively. Patience comes through the price of trials.

By analogy, the price we must pay for *physical* strength is to push ourselves past our comfort zone; to tax and stress our heart, lungs, and muscles beyond their normal tolerance; and to induce significant pain and fatigue. Then, afterward, by resting and nourishment our body recovers and becomes stronger than it was before.

This is also true of all *spiritual* progress, including patience. We must go through things that test and try us, that take us beyond our comfort zone, and that tax and stress us past our normal tolerance. Afterward, when the trial is over, we recover spiritually and become stronger than we were before.

- Peter said, in 1 Peter 5:10: "After you have suffered for a little while, the God of all grace, who called you to His eternal glory in Christ, will Himself perfect, confirm, strengthen and establish you."
- Peter also said, "For what credit is there if, when you sin and are harshly treated, you endure it with patience? But if when you do what is right and suffer for it you patiently endure it, this finds favor with God" (1 Peter 2:20).
- James instructs us: "Consider it all joy, my brothers and sisters, when you encounter various trials, knowing that the testing of your faith produces endurance" (1:2–3).
- James further encourages us: "As an example . . . of suffering and patience, take the prophets who spoke in the name of the Lord. We count those blessed who endured. You have heard of the endurance of Job and have seen the outcome of the Lord's dealings, that the Lord is full of compassion and is merciful" (5:10–11).

While trials are the price for developing patience, God is ready to meet us on the other side of these trials with spiritual growth and blessing.

5. Spiritual maturity is the reward of patience.

Spiritual m_____ is the reward of patience.

Finally, we come to the reward of endurance: "And let endurance have its perfect result, so that you may be perfect and complete, lacking in nothing" (James 1:4).

Who wouldn't want to be perfect and complete? But the only way to get there is on the other side of trials.

The word *perfect* here does not mean without imperfection. Rather, it means perfect in the sense of being complete and mature. When a kernel of corn is planted into soil, it eventually sends down roots, sprouts a fragile seedling, and then grows, *matures*, into the same thing that the seed came from. That's what it means to be "perfect": being fully formed, having become that which was intended.

Endurance, when fully formed into patience, can give us a stability, a fortitude, and a "centeredness" that makes life easier to live. Benjamin Franklin once wrote, "Discontentment makes a rich man poor while contentment makes a poor man rich." John Bunyan also said, "If we have not 'quiet' in our minds, outward comfort will do no more for us than a golden slipper on a gouty foot."

Trials, rightly endured, produce patience and other fruit of the Spirit. In Galatians 5:22–23 we read, "The fruit of the Spirit is love, joy, peace, patience . . ." When we have that fruit, we enter into a satisfaction in life that we cannot experience any other way.

Conclusion

Peter said, "Prepare your minds for action, keep sober *in spirit*, set your hope completely on the grace to be brought to you at the revelation of Jesus Christ" (1 Peter 1:13). Paul adds, "Therefore, if you have been raised up with Christ, keep seeking the things that are above, where Christ is, seated at the right hand of God. Set your mind on the things that are above, not on the things that are on earth" (Colossians 3:1–2).

We are to have an eternal perspective on life, viewing life as God does. Based on that eternal perspective, we can learn to endure the trials of life with more and more patience, becoming mature in our faith.

James Packer explains, "Patience means living out the belief that God orders everything for the spiritual good of his children. Patience does not just grin and bear things, stoic-like, but accepts them . . . as therapeutic workouts planned by a heavenly trainer who is resolved to get you up to full fitness."

William Barclay said something similar:

All kinds of experiences will come to us. There will be the test of the sorrows and the disappointments which seek to take our faith away. There will be the test of the seductions which seek to lure us from the right way. There will be the tests of the dangers, the sacrifices, the unpopularity which the Christian way must so often involve. But they are not meant to make us fall; they are meant to make us soar. They are not meant to defeat us; they are meant to be defeated. They are not meant to make us weaker; they are meant to make us stronger. Therefore we should not bemoan them; we should rejoice in them. The Christian is like the athlete. The heavier the course of training he undergoes, the more he is glad, because he knows that it is fitting him all the better for victorious effort.[1]

So let us mentally transfer our citizenship to heaven (where it *already* actually is) and lean into the trials of life.

We can use the five "patience hacks" for dealing with life irritations, and we can nurture an eternal perspective for cultivating patience during life's hard times.

SO, DON'T SINK YOUR OWN SHIP.
PAY THE PRICE TO BE PATIENT.

Don't Sink Your Own Ship

CHAPTER REVIEW

Repetition is the key to mental ownership.

You must be willing to give up a dime today to gain a dollar tomorrow.

1. Patience is a v_____.
2. Patience is required for life i_____.
3. Patience is required for the h_____ experiences of life.
4. Patience is developed through t_____.
5. Spiritual m_____ is the reward of patience.

DON'T SINK YOUR OWN SHIP

If something is important, you must repeat it until it changes you.

Chapter Summaries

1. Look to God for h_____.
2. R_____ q_____ when you sin.
3. Be totally o_____ to God.
4. Be a good s_____ of life's resources.
5. Be a s_____ to others.
6. Choose the f_____ of self-discipline.
7. Don't let m_____ become m_____.
8. G_____ your mind to g_____ your life.
9. Use your tongue to h_____, not to h_____.
10. Trust God's definition of s_____.
11. Keep your c_____ clear.
12. Nurture your r_____.
13. Pay the p_____ to be patient.

LIFE-CHECK

Answer these questions, either individually by journaling the answer or in a spiritual accountability group.

1. What experience can you remember in which you were impatient and made an emotional decision that you ended up regretting?

2. What experience have you seen in other people's lives in which they made a rash decision that turned out badly?

3. What situation are you facing right now in which you could be in danger of losing patience and making an emotional decision that you might regret later? What can you do to ensure you make a good decision?

4. Which of the five "patience hacks" do you find most helpful? Which one do you find least helpful?

5. What principle do you find most helpful in cultivating patience for life's truly hard situations?

 FOR FURTHER REFLECTION

Additional Scripture.

Proverbs 15:14   2 Corinthians 4:16–18
1 Corinthians 9:24–27   Colossians 3:1–3

 RESOURCES

For further study.

30 Days to Growing in Your Faith (Chapters 12, 23), Max Anders
Walking with God through Pain and Suffering, Timothy Keller

CHAPTER 14

ACCEPT THAT WITHOUT PAIN THERE IS NO GAIN

DON'T SINK YOUR OWN SHIP.
ACCEPT THAT WITHOUT PAIN THERE IS NO GAIN.

The road to transformation always goes through the tunnel of trials.

Consider it all joy, my brothers and sisters, when you encounter various trials, knowing that the testing of your faith produces endurance. And let endurance have its perfect result, so that you may be perfect and complete, lacking in nothing.
—JAMES 1:2-4

I had a root canal done in Colorado Springs. It was your worst dental nightmare realized.

We were living in Austin, Texas, at the time, and my wife and I had taken a driving vacation to Jackson Hole, Wyoming, hitting the highlights along the way: Rocky Mountain National Park, the Grand Tetons, and Yellowstone and Old Faithful. As we visited these spectacular sites, my teeth were the last thing I was thinking about.

But coming out of Jackson Hole on our way home, I began to

feel a mild pulse in my lower left molar that grew into a throb by the time we reached Cheyenne, Wyoming. As we turned south on I-25, the throbbing intensified into a great crescendo of pain by the time we hit Colorado Springs. We found a dentist (a diabolical sadist) who first had to find out which one of my teeth was really causing the problem (I told him twenty times) and how bad it was (it was killing me!). After shooting liquid oxygen on the tooth, creating enough pain to qualify me for a Purple Heart, he had to shoot me so full of Novocain to deaden the pain that my kneecaps went to sleep. I had felt nothing but agony for a day, and then I felt nothing at all for the next day.

We eventually made it home, and the experience eventually faded from my memory. But, at the time, it was a nightmare!

Prior to that incident, I had seen my dentist every six months for a cleaning and checkup. There was no hint that I would have any trouble. Why did I have to have tooth trouble while on vacation? Why couldn't it have been discovered at my last checkup? Why this? Why now? In retrospect it was a little thing, but it is a parable of many things in life. We hurt, often unexpectedly, and we don't understand why.

One of my favorite stories when I was growing up was the vintage Disney classic *Old Yeller*, the story of a pioneer family carving out an existence on the edge of wilderness. They adopt a huge "old yeller" dog, who then saves one of their sons from a pack of wild pigs.

The dog lives as a beloved member of the family until it once again saves their lives during an attack by a rabid wolf. In the process Old Yeller contracts rabies himself, and the lovable, lop-eared mutt is reduced to a snarling, drooling set of teeth. One of the boys was faced with the incomprehensible task of having to shoot the dog that had twice saved his life.

Afterward, in a tearjerking scene, the father tries to console the son on the loss of his dog—a blow that the whole family felt. I'll never forget the tender words of wisdom the boy's father gave: "Now and then, for no good reason a man can figure out, life will just haul off and knock him flat. Slam him agin' the ground so hard it seems like all his insides is busted. . . . But I'll tell you a trick that's sometimes a big help. Start looking around for something good to take the place of the bad. As a general rule, you can find it."[1]

How true that is! Difficult trials have happened to all of us. Life hauls off and socks us one right in the stomach, and we stand there, immobilized by the searing pain, doubled over, mouth agape, unable to breathe spiritually or emotionally. Questions flood our minds: *Why me? Why this? Why now? Does God care? Where is God when it hurts?*

The reality is, there is no easy answer. A Christian must stand nose-to-nose with this mind-bending truth: "A good God allows His children to suffer." Period. We can speculate on the reasons. We can ponder the consequences. We can debate the rationale. But the two towering truths remain unchanged: God is good, and His children suffer.

Though we may never fully understand why, *the road to transformation always goes through the tunnel of trials.*

If you are on a road that does not include trials, it is not the road to transformation. God wants us to be changed into the character likeness of Christ, and He often uses pain to accomplish it.

The central passage in Scripture on this theme is James 1:2–4, where we read: "Consider it all joy, my brothers and sisters, when you encounter various trials, knowing that the testing of your faith produces endurance. And let endurance have its perfect result, so that you may be perfect and complete, lacking in nothing."

From this passage, we learn five key truths about trials.

1. Trials are unavoidable—they come to everyone.

Trials are u_____—they come to everyone.

Trials happen to all of us—if not now, then later. Someone once said, "There are three different kinds of people: those who are in the middle of a trial, those who are going into a trial, and those who have just come out of a trial." James said to count it all joy *when*, not *if*, trials come your way.

I once heard the story of a man who was on his way home from work on the subway. He was prone to motion sickness, he had eaten a big lunch that didn't agree with him, he had worked hard all afternoon in a stuffy conference room, and he boarded the subway with an upset stomach. He was jammed into the train—the last person to get on—and the automatic door closed right at the end of his nose. He stood there, facing out the windows of the closed doors, things flashing by at ninety miles an hour. The longer he stayed in that spot, the sicker he got.

The train pulled up to the next stop, but the man did not want to get off. However, the train was so full that no one could get on, even though a small crowd was pressed up near the slowing train. The lurching and jerking of the stopping train was the last straw. The door opened, and up came this man's lunch all over the first man waiting on the platform. The door closed without anyone getting on or off, and the train sped on down the track. The unfortunate man whose chest had become the depository for the sick man's lunch turned to the person standing next to him, raised his palms to the heavens, and cried, "Why me?"

Sooner or later the doors of life open, someone's lunch is deposited on our chest, and we cry, "Why me?" James answers this question: it is not just you; it is everyone. If not now, then later—but everyone.

2. Trials make us spiritually strong.

Trials make us spiritually s_____.

We wish we could become spiritually strong by eating chocolate while watching beautiful sunsets. But that's not the way it works. James said, "Count it all joy . . . knowing that the testing of your faith produces endurance." The Greek word for "testing" implies a test designed to validate or refine the finished product.

When gold is dug out of the hills in its natural state, it's mixed with clay, iron ore, mineral deposits, and other impurities. To purify the gold, all the ore is put into huge vats and heated to a white-hot temperature until the whole mess bubbles like golden oatmeal. Gold is heavy, so in this liquefied state all the gold settles to the bottom and everything that is not gold rises to the top, like ugly froth. This stuff is called *dross*. The dross is skimmed off, and what is left behind is pure gold.

Without the heat there would be no separation of the gold from the impurities. In the same way, trials can be used to separate us from our personal impurities. This is the process the writer of the hymn "How Firm a Foundation" was referring to when he wrote:

> When through fiery trials thy pathway shall lie,
> My grace, all sufficient, shall be thy supply;
> The flame shall not hurt thee; I only design
> Thy dross to consume and thy gold to refine.

It's the same as when a blacksmith works with a horseshoe. He holds it in the fire to heat and soften it and make it malleable. Then, with blows from a hammer, he shapes it into what is needed. That is why God permits the testing of our faith by trials. He wants us to become spiritually malleable.

3. Trials can change us into the character image of Christ.

Trials can change us into the c_____ image of Christ.

The one who "endures" remains under refinement in God's fire until God's work in him is done. Then we become "perfect and complete, lacking in nothing." If we are to become all that God wants us to become, we must endure the pain and remain spiritually sensitive, obedient, and faithful.

When we remain faithful to God in trials, we become "perfect." Perfect does not mean without flaw. Rather, it means "complete, mature, fully developed." It means we become mature in our character. "Complete" carries with it the idea of being whole. "Lacking in nothing," then, would have the idea of not being void of any major character qualities.

There may be times in the life of a Christian when the grace of God does not seem sufficient to bear the suffering. We may be willing to believe that God has a purpose in this trial, but we just want to know how to survive.

Even Jesus Himself experienced suffering that took Him beyond a calm peace. He was deeply "grieved and distressed" in the garden of Gethsemane before His betrayal and crucifixion, saying to His disciples, "My soul is deeply grieved, to the point of death . . . and He went a little beyond them, and fell on His face and prayed" (Matthew 26:37–39). Luke records that "being in agony, He was praying very fervently; and His sweat became like drops of blood, falling down upon the ground" (Luke 22:44). Later, on the cross, Jesus cried, "My God, My God, why have You forsaken Me?" (Matthew 27:46).

We see then that, even in the life of our Lord, suffering was real, and the grace of God did not take away His pain. Nor did the grace of God make it easy to endure. But the grace of God did make the suffering (just barely) endurable.

In the middle of suffering, many of us would say that the grace of God does not seem sufficient. But when we look back, we see that, somehow, He did sustain us. The grace of God doesn't always enable us to go water skiing through life. Sometimes it just keeps our nostrils above the surface of the water enough of the time.

The road to transformation always goes through the tunnel of trials. It is important to remember what James 1:2–4 teaches us:

- Trials are unavoidable—they will come to us all.
- Trials make us spiritually strong.
- Trials can change us into the character image of Christ.

4. God will convert our suffering into spiritual blessing.

God will convert our suffering into spiritual b_____.

Terry Waite, former emissary to the archbishop of Canterbury, went to the Middle East in 1986 to try to negotiate the release of some hostages who had been taken by terrorists, and ended up a hostage himself. He was released at the end of 1991 after nearly five years of solitary confinement in Lebanon, chained to the wall of his room for almost twenty-four hours a day.

After his release, he wrote: "I have been determined in captivity, and still am determined, to convert this experience into something that will be useful and good for other people. I think that's the way to approach suffering. It seems to me that Christianity doesn't in any way lessen suffering. What it does is enable you to take it, face it, to work through it, and eventually to convert it."

Daniel Defoe wrote in *Robinson Crusoe*, a book filled with deep spiritual insights, that "God will often deliver us in a manner that seems, initially, to bring about our destruction." It is often only after we think we have been destroyed—and survived—that we begin to believe this profound truth and draw spiritual strength from it.

In a more elaborate expression, the hymnwriter John Newton wrote in an untitled poem:

> I asked the Lord that I might grow
> In faith and love and every grace;
> Might more of his salvation know,
> And seek more earnestly his face.

'Twas he who taught me thus to pray,
And he, I trust, has answered prayer;
But it has been in such a way
As almost drove me to despair.

I hoped that in some favored hour
At once he'd answer my request,
And by his love's constraining power
Subdue my sins, and give me rest.

Instead of this, he made me feel
The hidden evil of my heart,
And let the angry powers of hell
Assault my soul in every part.

Yea, more, with his own hand he seemed
Intent to aggravate my woe,
Crossed all the fair designs I schemed,
Blasted my gourds, and laid me low.

"Lord, why this?" I trembling cried,
"Wilt thou pursue thy worm to death?"
"'Tis in this way," the Lord replied,
"I answer prayer for grace and faith.

These inward trials I employ
From self and pride to set thee free,
And break thy schemes of earthly joy,
That thou mayest seek thy all in me."

God will convert our suffering into spiritual blessing if we trust Him.

5. We can draw additional strength from Jesus's example of suffering for us.

We can draw additional strength from Jesus's e_____ of suffering for us.

James Packer, in his book *Rediscovering Holiness*, admitted his own need for help during times of intense suffering: "I am a silly child who stumbles and fumbles and tumbles every day. Holy Father, Holy Son, Holy Spirit, I need Your help. Lord, have mercy; hold me up, and hold me steady—please, starting now. Amen."[2]

The first time I read *Rediscovering Holiness* was during a time of significant physical suffering. I didn't feel like I was going through it very well. The grace of God didn't seem sufficient. Day after day, week after week, and month after month, I pleaded with God to bring me relief from my suffering, to make His grace sufficient for me. Each night, I prayed that God would make tomorrow a better day. And, for months at a time, tomorrow was no better; it was often worse.

I did not feel, on many occasions, that even my nostrils were above the surface. But by some miracle of grace that I can only see looking backward, God saw me through.

We can draw additional strength from Jesus's example of suffering for us. Our bond with Jesus is strengthened by observing that He suffered more for us than we suffer for Him, a fact that is magnified by the realization that *His suffering was caused by our sin—and He willingly suffered to pay for our sin.*

As Edward Shillito wrote in his poem, "Jesus of the Scars":

> The other gods were strong, but You were weak.
> They rode, but You stumbled to the throne.
> But to our wounds only God's wounds can speak,
> And no god has wounds but You alone.

Jesus willingly entered our world of suffering, and as a result, "We do not have a high priest who cannot sympathize with our weaknesses, but One who has been tempted in all things as *we are, yet* without sin. Therefore let's approach the throne of grace with confidence, so that we may receive mercy and find grace for help at the time of our need" (Hebrews 4:15–16).

The door is wide open to go to Jesus for grace and strength when we are suffering.

Conclusion

The hottest fire produces the strongest steel. The wildest winds make the toughest trees. The greatest trials create the strongest faith. Wanting to be a mature Christian without trials is like wanting to be a great athlete without training, to be pure gold without refining, or to be an accomplished pianist without the practice.

Certainly, if the suffering is significant, we will want to escape. If the trial is not something that makes us want to escape, then it is not intense enough to strengthen the steel, toughen the tree, condition the athlete, purify the gold, or prepare the pianist.

There is no embarrassment in wanting to escape; even Moses, even the apostle Paul, and even Jesus wanted to escape. But often we can't. So, in the midst of our pain, we remind ourselves, *God has not abandoned us. This will bring about for us the transformation we long for.*

When you are crying for release is when you're being most fitted by God for great character and service. When the pain seems unbearable, we cry out to God as Jesus did for the grace to bear it. We take hope in the fact that the season of suffering will produce great spiritual growth and great eternal reward.

Suffering is a calling for each Christian—one that prepares us for glory with Christ by drawing us deeper into the sanctity of being like Him. And, of course, we fulfill our purpose imperfectly. Yet, if someone the stature of Packer can say, "I am a silly child who stumbles and fumbles and tumbles every day," then we need not despair if we stumble and fumble and tumble. But, let us also pray along with him: "Holy Father, Holy Son, Holy Spirit, I need Your help. Lord, have mercy; hold me up, and hold me steady—please, starting now. Amen."

So, DON'T SINK YOUR OWN SHIP.

ACCEPT THAT WITHOUT PAIN THERE IS NO GAIN.

CHAPTER REVIEW

Repetition is the key to mental ownership.

The road to transformation always goes through the tunnel of trials.

1. Trials are u_____—they come to everyone.
2. Trials make us spiritually s_____.
3. Trials can change us into the c_____ image of Christ.
4. God will convert our suffering into spiritual b_____.
5. We can draw additional strength from Jesus's e_____ of suffering for us.

DON'T SINK YOUR OWN SHIP

If something is important, you must repeat it until it changes you.

Chapter Summaries

1. Look to God for h_____.
2. R_____ q_____ when you sin.
3. Be totally o_____ to God.
4. Be a good s_____ of life's resources.
5. Be a s_____ to others.
6. Choose the f_____ of self-discipline.
7. Don't let m_____ become m_____.
8. G_____ your mind to g_____ your life.
9. Use your tongue to h_____, not to h_____.
10. Trust God's definition of s_____.
11. Keep your c_____ clear.
12. Nurture your r_____.
13. Pay the p_____ to be patient.
14. Accept that without p_____ there is no g_____.

LIFE-CHECK

Answer these questions, either individually by journaling the answer or in a spiritual accountability group.

1. What trial are you experiencing now that is at the top of your list? Have you prayed for insight into why you are experiencing this trial? Have you gained the insight you want?

2. Recall my words, "God will often deliver us in a manner that seems, initially, to bring about our destruction." Have you gone through an experience like this? Can you transfer the insight you gained from it to the number one trial you are facing today?

3. What is the greatest area of spiritual strength you need in life? What are some ways you can see how your biggest trial will give you that kind of strength?

4. What spiritual insight and ministry do you think you will be able to share with others as a result of this trial?

 FOR FURTHER REFLECTION

Additional Scripture.

Matthew 26:37–39   2 Corinthians 12:7–9
Matthew 27:46   James 1:2–4
Luke 22:44   1 Peter 1:6–9
1 Corinthians 10:13   1 Peter 4:12–16
2 Corinthians 1:8–10

 RESOURCES

For further study.

30 Days to Growing in Your Faith (Chapters 12, 23), Max Anders
Walking with God through Pain and Suffering, Timothy Keller
Rediscovering Holiness, James Packer

CHAPTER 15

RENEW YOUR MIND TO TRANSFORM YOUR LIFE

DON'T SINK YOUR OWN SHIP.
RENEW YOUR MIND TO TRANSFORM YOUR LIFE.

If something is important, we must repeat it until it changes us.

Do not be conformed to this world, but be transformed by the
renewing of your mind, so that you may prove what the will of
God is, that which is good and acceptable and perfect.
—ROMANS 12:2

Every moment of every day, something in our soul is being fed
and something is being starved. Because we live in a media-
dominated world, and because much of what comes through that
media is an assault on biblical values, then in the course of living
everyday life the soul of the Christian is power-fed the things of the
world while the things of the spirit are starved.

As a result, Christians are being swept out to sea by the riptide
of modern culture.

Therefore, one of the great needs for Christendom in the twenty-first century is to devise a way to power-feed the things of the Spirit to the soul sufficiently to offset the things of the world.

Fortunately, new information from the world of neuroscience tells us that we do not have to offset twelve hours of input from the world with twelve hours of input from the Spirit. In fact, research tells us that as little as fifteen minutes a day of concentrated, focused mental attention is sufficient to offset the subconscious conditioning from the world.

Therefore, Christians must give focused, concentrated attention to the truth that will offset the subconscious conditioning of the world. This starts with what we truly believe.

1. What we believe controls everything about us.

What we b_____ controls everything about us.

The desire to be happy is the highest desire of the human heart. Let me repeat the insight of Blaise Pascal I shared in chapter 1:

> All men seek happiness. This is without exception. Whatever different means they employ, they all tend to this end. The cause of some going to war, and of others avoiding it, is the same desire in both, attended with different views. The will never takes the least step but to this object. This is the motive of every action of every man, even of those who hang themselves.[1]

Whatever we truly believe will make us happy is what controls us.

However, the brain does not necessarily believe what is true. Often it believes what it hears first, or what it hears most often, leading us to believe things that are not true.

What we hear early and often typically shapes us for the rest of our lives. Our family, our early education, our early friends, our early experiences, and our culture tend to form the beliefs that guide us through adulthood. The process is largely automatic and subconscious.

Generally, we do not realize that the subconscious brain is responsible for the majority of our thinking. In an article in *Scientific American*, we read, "We are aware of a tiny fraction of the thinking that goes on in our minds, and we can control only a tiny part of our conscious thoughts. The vast majority of our thinking efforts goes on subconsciously."[2]

This reality helped us in the earlier days of our national history when biblical principles heavily influenced our culture. Automatically and subconsciously, we took on biblical values that shaped us positively. But as American culture has devolved, gradually degrading from biblical to non-biblical values, it now works against us in deeply negative ways.

As a result, Christians often subconsciously take on non-biblical values even while they consciously espouse biblical values.

In a *New York Times* article titled "Who's Minding the Mind?" we read,

> We're finding that we have these unconscious behavioral guidance systems that are continually furnishing suggestions through the day about what to do next, and the brain is considering and often acting on those, all before conscious awareness. *Sometimes those goals are in line with our conscious intentions and purposes, and sometimes they're not.* (emphasis added)[3]

As a result, Christians are beginning to pursue the same non-biblical avenues for personal happiness that the world is pursuing—often while consciously espousing biblical values.

This leads us to unbiblical attitudes, values, and behavior which are inherently self-destructive and which the Bible calls us to abandon in favor of biblical attitudes, values, and behavior.

2. Mental renewal is a make-or-break issue in the Christian life.

Mental r_____ is a make-or-break issue in the Christian life.

We cannot thrive spiritually while embracing temporal values. So we must find ways to renew our minds, which is the key to transforming our lives.

Romans 12:2 addresses this critical issue:

> Do not be conformed to this world, but be transformed by the renewing of your mind, so that you may prove what the will of God is, that which is good and acceptable and perfect.

This tells us three things:

- We can be living demonstrations of the fact that God's will is good and acceptable and perfect.
- This only happens if we are transformed.
- In order to be transformed, our minds must be renewed.

Therefore, mental renewal is the make-or-break, sink-or-swim, do-or-die issue for motivated Christians.

3. We can become our own brain surgeon.

We can become our own b_____ s_____.

Contrary to what science used to believe, we now know that the brain can change, and does change, and always changes in the direction of what is put into it.

Therefore, to offset what has inevitably been put into the brain from the world around us, we can choose to replace the lies and unhelpful input from the world with truth and helpful input from Scripture. This is self-directed neuroplasticity (neuro = brain, plasticity = change).

There are 100,000 miles of electrical wiring in the brain. Every time we think a thought, it takes the same pathway in the brain. Much like wearing a pathway in grass, our thinking a thought over and over creates a deeper and deeper path in the brain. As a result, a triggered thought takes the path of least resistance in the brain. So often, our first neurological response is the one burned into our brain from the world around us, beginning at a very early age.

But if we think the right thoughts (concentrated, focused attention) over and over, we can wear new pathways in the brain that allow the brain to more and more frequently take the new and right path.

As new, helpful pathways are deepened and older, unhelpful pathways are neglected, we reach a tipping point in which it becomes easier for the brain to take the new path than the old one. And at that point, we experience a surge of spiritual growth that we cannot experience any other way.

God's Word urges us to guide and control our thinking, and to fill our minds with the truth of Scripture:

- "Meditate on it day and night" (Joshua 1:8).
- "Whatever is true, whatever is honorable, whatever is right, whatever is pure, whatever is lovely, whatever is commendable, if there is any excellence and if anything worthy of praise, think about these things" (Philippians 4:8).
- "[Take] every thought captive to the obedience of Christ" (2 Corinthians 10:5).

Scripture tells us what to do; neuroscience is shedding a floodlight on why we do it.

When you understand the power of your thought life . . . you truly begin to get a glimpse of how important it is to take responsibility for what you are thinking. God was so serious about us capturing our thoughts and renewing our minds that he gave us science as an encouragement.[4]

4. We feed our subconscious, and then our subconscious feeds us.

We f_____ our subconscious, and then our subconscious f_____ us.

Our subconscious mental activity significantly affects our conscious mental activity, even though we aren't aware of it. This happens in two ways.

First, the Reticular Activating System (RAS) kicks in and starts revealing to us information and truth that we didn't see before. The RAS is the doorkeeper for the brain; it determines what comes into our brains from the world around us, and what doesn't.

The RAS filters out most of what bombards the brain and only allows things through the doorway that have been identified as important. Once something has been identified as important, the RAS allows more information on that subject into the brain.

For example, I had never owned a black car before we bought one, not because it was black but because it was a bargain. So, frankly, I had never been particularly aware of black cars.

After I bought this car, however, I started seeing black cars everywhere. It seemed like half the cars on the road were black. Who knew? That was the RAS letting information into my brain that it was screening out before.

And the RAS does this on everything. For example, if you go to the doctor and learn for the first time that you have high blood pressure, it is very likely that you will begin to notice articles on blood pressure that you hadn't noticed before. The RAS will register that a drug advertisement on television which you hadn't paid any attention to before is for blood pressure, and you will notice an internet advertisement on an herb that helps lower blood pressure which you would not have noticed before.

So, when you feed your mind large amounts of truth by memorizing and meditating on Scripture, for example, your RAS will then start revealing to you a whole world of information and truth that you didn't notice before. It will make you more aware, feed you new information, and significantly raise your awareness and absorption of truth.

Second, your subconscious will prompt mental activity in your conscious brain.

As we saw earlier, **sometimes what we think on a conscious level is not the same as what we think on the subconscious level.** Sometimes what we are harboring in our subconscious is opposite of what we embrace in our conscious mind.

For example, the Bible tells us that we should love our neighbor. As Christians, we consciously recognize and embrace that truth. But subconsciously we may feel that it is a pain to always love, especially when our neighbor is a jerk. When our neighbor does something to demean us, we feel a conscious need to defend ourselves by putting our neighbor in his or her place. So we talk: "*love our neighbor*," but we act: "*protect ourselves*."

Therefore, because conscious values are often different from our subconscious values, **one of the great challenges for the Christian is to bring the attitudes, values, and behavior of the subconscious mind into harmony with the attitudes, values, and behavior of the conscious mind.** We can do that through repetition of the right information.

> Whatever you think about the most will grow, so the more you think a particular thought, the stronger it grows. You can't just apply a thought once and think change has happened.[5]

So, repetition drives truth deeply into our subconscious where it changes our fundamental attitudes, values, and behavior, and it is at this level that we are deeply changed.

In summary, when we repeat things often enough, the following actions happen:

1. The truth begins to come to the surface of our conscious thought, affecting our decisions and emotions. For example, when we get angry, we are enabled to recall verses and truth about anger and can use that information to help us keep from acting in anger.
2. Then, truth sinks deeply into the subconscious where it lodges as controlling beliefs and begins to alter our basic attitudes, values, and behavior. When this happens, it takes spiritual growth to a whole new level. Instead of enabling us on a conscious level not to act on anger, it now, on a subconscious level, changes us so that we don't get angry in the first place.
3. Truth also triggers our Reticular Activating System, the part of our brain that chooses what to let into the brain and what to keep out. As a result, we start perceiving truth that escaped us before. It creates new insights, revises estimates of importance, sees relative significance, and connects dots, making us more aware, insightful, and smarter.
4. Finally, the subconscious bubbles this mental gold back up to the conscious so we can also intentionally act on it, multiplying its power.

Conclusion

Felix Mendelssohn, the brilliant composer, had an astonishing memory and mental capacity. One of his most famous works is his *Overture to a Midsummer Night's Dream*, a dazzling composition still popular today. After he wrote it in 1829, he carelessly left the manuscript in a horse-drawn taxi in London and it disappeared. But he seemed curiously unconcerned about it.

The reason became evident when Mendelssohn sat down

and, astonishingly, wrote the overture out again from memory. Magnifying that feat, the lost manuscript turned up at the Royal Academy of Music some one hundred years later. When it was compared with the second manuscript, out of tens of thousands of notes there were no discrepancies!

This feat of memory is well beyond the capacity of mere mortals. Most of us identify more completely with a young man who had just witnessed the birth of his daughter. After the baby was cleaned up, the dad was allowed to hold her for just a few minutes before she needed to go back to her mother. As he did, tears welled up in his eyes. He drew a breath and opened his mouth to speak. His wife paused expectantly to hear something poetic in this tender moment. In response, the dad said, "What's her name again?"

Most of us identify more with the new father than with Mendelssohn.

Nevertheless, mental renewal and life transformation is within the grasp of all of us. As we feed our minds in episodes of concentrated, focused attention on biblical truth, that truth sinks deeply into our subconscious where it transforms our fundamental attitudes, values, and behavior, changing us from the inside out. As Romans 12:2 indicates, we can become living demonstrations of the fact that God's will is good and acceptable and perfect as we renew our mind, which transforms our life.

So, DON'T SINK YOUR OWN SHIP.
RENEW YOUR MIND TO TRANSFORM YOUR LIFE.

CHAPTER REVIEW

Repetition is the key to mental ownership.

If something is important, we must repeat it until it changes us.

1. What we b_____ controls everything about us.
2. Mental r_____ is a make-or-break issue in the Christian life.
3. We can become our own b_____ s_____.
4. We f_____ our subconscious, and then our subconscious f_____ us.

DON'T SINK YOUR OWN SHIP

If something is important, you must repeat it until it changes you.

Chapter Summaries

1. Look to God for h_____.
2. R_____ q_____ when you sin.
3. Be totally o_____ to God.
4. Be a good s_____ of life's resources.
5. Be a s_____ to others.
6. Choose the f_____ of self-discipline.
7. Don't let m_____ become m_____.
8. G_____ your mind to g_____ your life.
9. Use your tongue to h_____, not to h_____.
10. Trust God's definition of s_____.
11. Keep your c_____ clear.
12. Nurture your r_____.
13. Pay the p_____ to be patient.
14. Accept that without p_____ there is no g_____.
15. Renew your m_____ to transform your l_____.

186

LIFE-CHECK

Answer these questions, either individually by journaling the answer or in a spiritual accountability group.

1. Can you think of any attitudes, values, or behavior that you picked up subconsciously at an early age?

2. As you think about it, do any subjects come to mind in which you might have subconscious beliefs that are in conflict with your conscious biblical beliefs?

3. How important do you think mental renewal is in your life?

4. What changes do you think you should make to be your own brain surgeon?

 FOR FURTHER REFLECTION

Additional Scripture.

Joshua 1:8   Philippians 4:7

Proverbs 2:1–12   Philippians 4:8

2 Corinthians 10:5   Colossians 3:2

Ephesians 4:23

 RESOURCES

For further study.

30 Days to Growing in Your Faith (Chapters 6, 9), Max Anders

Brave New Discipleship, Max Anders

The Change Zone (www.thechangezone.com)

CHAPTER 16

DON'T PLAY CHECKERS WHILE GOD IS PLAYING CHESS

DON'T SINK YOUR OWN SHIP.
DON'T PLAY CHECKERS WHILE GOD IS PLAYING CHESS.

Walk by faith and not by sight.

If you have been raised with Christ, keep seeking the things
that are above, where Christ is, seated at the right hand of
God. Set your minds on the things that are above, not on the
things that are on earth.
—COLOSSIANS 3:1-2

The story is told of a time early in the U.S. space program, when
NASA scientists, in an effort to test the outer limits of human
physical capacities, fitted the astronauts with complex goggles con-
taining multiple lenses that turned their vision upside down.

Suddenly, up was down and right was left. Everything was
backward, and this made even the simplest tasks, such as walking
across the room, or eating, or getting dressed, almost impossible.

189

What their eyes told them was not merely wrong, but absolutely opposite.

In order to function even at a minimal level, the astronauts had to stop trusting their eyes, go into an inner world to "feel" what the right move should be, and trust their inner sense of reality rather than what they saw. They had to continuously force themselves to reject what they were seeing in favor of their inner conviction of reality.

What a powerful parable that is of an eternal perspective! Living in a fallen world controlled by the enemy of our souls, it feels like Christians have been fitted with spiritual goggles that turn the world upside down, making even the simplest spiritual tasks a significant challenge.

Scripture tells us that there are two worlds: the seen, physical, temporal world and the unseen, spiritual, eternal world.

These two worlds are in conflict.

1. In the seen world:
   - We walk by sight.
   - Truth is what I say it is.
   - Emotions are reliable.
   - Happiness is the highest good.
   - Happiness is achieved by following your heart.
2. In the unseen world:
   - We walk by faith.
   - Truth is what God says it is.
   - Emotions are not reliable.
   - Holiness is the highest good.
   - Happiness is achieved by following God.

These two sets of beliefs cannot both be true. Therefore, we must choose between them. This makes functioning according to an eternal perspective one of the central challenges of the Christian life.

With an eternal perspective, God makes sense, His will is reasonable, we rest in the fact that He loves us, and we place our hope in the future. With a temporal perspective, God does not make sense, His will is often unreasonable, we wonder if He loves us, and our hopes for this world are often frustrated.

So, when we are exasperated from living with an eternal perspective, truth says, "Well, no wonder. You are playing checkers while God is playing chess." Without an eternal perspective, we make all the wrong moves. In the end, we lose.

There are five components of an eternal perspective. If we know and embrace these five components, life will still be a challenge but is "doable." To the degree that we do not know or embrace these five components, life will typically beat us up one side and down the other, leaving us frustrated, discouraged, or possibly even defeated. Let's look at the five components.

1. Believe the unbelievable.

Believe the u_____.

 a. You must believe that God exists in spite of the absence of scientific proof.

 b. You must believe that God is good in spite of the rampant evil in the world.

 c. You must believe that God loves you in spite of the fact that He does not make your life go better.

C. S. Lewis once said, "When the whole world is running towards a cliff, anyone running in the opposite direction appears to have lost his mind."

There couldn't be a better description of a committed Christian. With a temporal perspective, the whole world is "running towards a cliff." The believer must run *away* from it. In doing so, he will look as though he has lost his mind.

So many things in Scripture are counterintuitive and take us 180 degrees in the opposite direction of our natural inclinations. That is why Scripture is so challenging.

When I say we must believe the unbelievable, it is not *really* unbelievable. It just *looks* that way at first glance. It looks that way to someone with a temporal perspective. On second glance, however, if we take all available evidence at face value and carry it to its logical conclusion, the unbelievable is the only thing that *can* be believed.

For that reason, it is "believable" that God exists, that He is good in spite of all the rampant evil in the world, and that He loves us in spite of the fact that He does not make our lives go better.

It is not within the purpose or scope of this book to answer each of the three issues I just mentioned, but there are powerful and convincing arguments for them, and Christians need not fear their credibility. Rather, we must embrace them as the only truly believable things to embrace. As we embrace them, we take our first step in conforming to an eternal perspective.

2. Embrace the inconceivable.

Embrace the i_____.

  a. You must accept your redeemed inner man as holy and righteous.
  b. You must accept your inherent worth as a child of God.
  c. You must recognize God as your only source of ultimate happiness.

It is not *truly* inconceivable that Christians are holy and righteous (Ephesians 4:24), that we have inherent worth as children of God (Ephesians 1:4–5), and that God is our only source of ultimate happiness (Psalm 16:11).

But just as Satan whispered in Eve's ear, causing her to doubt God's total sufficiency for her happiness, so he whispers in ours. And just as Eve believed Satan and acted accordingly, so do we often believe him and act accordingly.

But the eyes of faith trust and accept the "inconceivable," resting in our worth in God's eyes and His sufficiency for our happiness.

3. Choose the undesirable.

Choose the u_____.

   a. You must choose God over personal happiness.
   b. You must choose others over self.
   c. You must choose the eventual over the immediate.

Again, these things are not truly undesirable. They just appear to be undesirable to the earthly mind and heart. The reality is, happiness for a Christian is not achieved by pursuing happiness; it is achieved by pursuing God. Plus, as Benjamin Disraeli said, "We are born for love. It is the principle of existence and its only end." To have "others" to love and to have "others" love us is the key to happiness in this world. And when we choose others over self, they are encouraged to reciprocate, setting the stage for truly rewarding relationships.

Finally, to choose the eventual over the immediate is a fundamental mark of maturity. In the well-known Stanford marshmallow experiment, researchers offered children either one marshmallow now or two marshmallows later if they waited. They recorded which children waited and which ones didn't, and then followed them for the next twenty years. They found that the children who waited for two marshmallows were happier and more successful in life. Thus, choosing the eventual over the immediate demonstrates maturity and maximizes God's blessing and reward in our lives.

4. Fight the invisible.

Fight the i_____.

    a. Alert: You must be alert to the reality of spiritual warfare.

    b. Armor: You must choose spiritual weapons for spiritual conflict.

    c. Resist: You must be shrewd in detecting spiritual deception and you must not take the bait.

Scripture makes it clear that all Christians fight a continuous spiritual battle (Ephesians 6:10–17; 1 Peter 5:8; James 4:7). Regarding this reality, C. S. Lewis said, "There are two equal and opposite errors into which our race can fall about the devils. One is to disbelieve in their existence. The other is to believe, and to feel an excessive and unhealthy interest in them. They themselves are equally pleased by both errors and hail a materialist or a magician with the same delight."

Lewis also said, "Every square inch in the universe and every split second of time is claimed by God and counter claimed by Satan."

This all suggests that spiritual warfare is not occasional but constant. One of the most important mental shifts a Christian must make is the shift from living for the American Dream to fighting the spiritual battle. This is one of the major mental shifts a person must make if he or she is to have an adequate eternal perspective. Falling short on this point sets yourself up for disappointment and discouragement.

5. Nurture the transformational.

Nurture the t_____.

    a. You must carefully manage what you believe.

    b. You must use your mind to change your brain.

    c. You must repeat truth until it changes you.

As we mentioned in Chapter 15, mental renewal is a make-or-break, sink-or-swim, do-or-die issue in the Christian life. Christians are being swept out to sea by the riptide of modern culture. Romans 12:2 tells us that we can be living demonstrations of the fact that God's will is good and acceptable and perfect, but only if we are transformed. And we will be transformed only as our minds are renewed. If we nurture the transformational, we can complete the five steps to a robust eternal perspective.

So, as we said at the beginning, there are five components of an eternal perspective. If we know and embrace these five components, life will still be a challenge, but it is "doable." To the degree that we do not know or embrace these five components, life will leave us frustrated, discouraged, or possibly even defeated.

SO, DON'T SINK YOUR OWN SHIP.
DON'T PLAY CHECKERS WHILE GOD IS PLAYING CHESS.

CHAPTER REVIEW

Repetition is the key to mental ownership.

Walk by faith and not by sight.

1. Believe the u_____.
2. Embrace the i_____.
3. Choose the u_____.
4. Fight the i_____.
5. Nurture the t_____.

 DON'T SINK YOUR OWN SHIP

If something is important, you must repeat it until it changes you.

Chapter Summaries

1. Look to God for h_____.
2. R_____ q_____ when you sin.
3. Be totally o_____ to God.
4. Be a good s_____ of life's resources.
5. Be a s_____ to others.
6. Choose the f_____ of self-discipline.
7. Don't let m_____ become m_____.
8. G_____ your mind to g_____ your life.
9. Use your tongue to h_____, not to h_____.
10. Trust God's definition of s_____.
11. Keep your c_____ clear.
12. Nurture your r_____.
13. Pay the p_____ to be patient.
14. Accept that without p_____ there is no g_____.
15. Renew your m_____ to transform your l_____.
16. Don't play c_____ while God is playing c_____.

LIFE-CHECK

Answer these questions, either individually by journaling the answer or in a spiritual accountability group.

1. How do you rate yourself (1–10) on believing the unbelievable?
2. How do you rate yourself (1–10) on embracing the inconceivable?
3. How do you rate yourself (1–10) on choosing the undesirable?
4. How do you rate yourself (1–10) on fighting the invisible?
5. How do you rate yourself (1–10) on nurturing the transformational?
6. What step(s) do you think you should/could take in each of these areas?

 FOR FURTHER REFLECTION

Additional Scripture.

Mark 10:45   Ephesians 4:24
Romans 1:18–32   Ephesians 6:10–18
Romans 12:2

 RESOURCE

For further study.

30 Days to Growing in Your Faith (Chapter 2), Max Anders

CHAPTER 17

TRUST FACTS TO
GUIDE YOUR LIFE

DON'T SINK YOUR OWN SHIP.
TRUST FACTS TO GUIDE YOUR LIFE.

Truth is true, no matter what you think, believe, or feel.

You will know the truth, and the truth will set you free.
—JOHN 8:32

I read one time of a liar's club in Burlington, Wisconsin, that you could join for $1.00 and a good enough lie. Some of the stories people submitted to get into the liar's club were doozies! One man said his wife's feet were so cold that every time she took her shoes off the furnace kicked on. Another man said he was fishing one day where the fish were biting so well that he had to stand behind a tree to bait his hook. Someone else said he cut a tree down on a day when it was so foggy the tree didn't fall over until the fog lifted.

A gentleman from Alabama looked over the national registry of the liar's club and discovered there were liars listed from every state in the Union except Alabama. He wrote to the liar's club to make that notable observation, and then added that that was because there *were* no liars in Alabama. The liar's club was so deeply impressed that they gave him a free lifetime membership!

Sometimes life *sounds* like a tall tale, but isn't. I once read a story involving Beverly Sills, one of the great operatic sopranos of the twentieth century. She said that when she was first trying to break into the world of opera, she got a job traveling to remote rural areas of the United States bringing culture to places that would otherwise be unable to have it.

She was scheduled to go to a very small town in the middle of Nebraska where, coincidentally, the residents were having a serious outbreak of a cattle disease called *stinking smut.* The local paper unfortunately got the pictures and the captions of the two events mixed up on its front page. Beneath the picture of a sick cow was the caption "Beverly Sills to sing locally." Beneath the picture of Beverly Sills was the caption "Stinking smut hits Nebraska!"

The difference between a lie and a tall tale is that no one is supposed to know a lie is a lie, but *everyone* knows that a tall tale is not true. Lying is wrong. Tall tales are just good fun.

1. Truth is that which conforms to reality.

Truth is that which conforms to r_____.

Truth is equal to "what is." Therefore, truth is true whether we know it or not, and whether we believe it or not.

Truth is relentless and all-powerful. You cannot change truth any more than you can defy gravity. Therefore, Christians must be people of the truth . . . people who know the truth, believe the truth, and live the truth.

- Columnist William F. Buckley Jr. once famously said, "The beginning of wisdom is the fear of the Lord. The next and most urgent counsel is to take stock of reality."

- Churchill once wrote: "The truth is incontrovertible. Malice may attack it, ignorance may deride it, but in the end, there it is."
- Einstein said: "Whoever is careless with the truth in small matters cannot be trusted in important affairs."

Look at the emphasis Scripture places on truth:

- John 3:33 says, "God is true."
- Romans 3:4 says, "God must prove to be true, though every person be found a liar."
- John 17:17 says, "Sanctify them in the truth; Your word is truth."
- John 14:6 says, "I am the way, and the truth, and the life;"
- John 8:32 says, "You will know the truth, and the truth will set you free."

As we said, truth is that which conforms to reality. Truth is equal to "what is." Therefore, truth is true whether we know it or not, and whether we believe it or not.

However, years ago, Allan Bloom in his landmark book *The Closing of the American Mind* stated that the single most agreed-upon truth on the American campus today is that truth is relative—that there is no such thing as absolute truth. Rather, each person is free to determine what is true for him/herself. You may believe one thing is true, and I believe the opposite, but that's okay because each thing is true to the one who believes it.[1]

In 2016, the Oxford Dictionary named *post-truth* its word of the year. According to its definition, post-truth is "relating to or denoting circumstances in which objective facts are less influential in shaping public opinion than appeals to emotion and personal belief."

Thus, in a post-truth world people are guided by subjective

feelings rather than objective facts. American culture is now saying, "Speaking your truth is the most powerful tool we all have."[2] We say "*your* truth," instead of "*the* truth."

"What's true for you doesn't have to be true for me" is the mantra of the post-truth age. This is preposterous. It is a fundamental tenet of reality that something cannot be A and non-A at the same time. And yet vast segments of our population, particularly reflecting those educated in the last few decades, are giving themselves over to this previously unthinkable perspective, wreaking havoc in government, education, business, social media, entertainment, and throughout American culture.

2. Truth has become a choice between facts and feelings.

Truth has become a choice between f_____ and f_____.

Sometimes things are stated as *true* which everyone knows is a subjective *preference*. To say "Italian food is the best!" is a subjective statement. Someone else may prefer French or American or Mexican . . . and so would not agree with the Italian food claim. We all understand that. It's *subjective truth*—"true for you, but not necessarily true for me."

On the other hand, there is *objective truth*. "The sky is blue" or "the grass is green" or "two plus two equals four" are all statements of objective truth. They are factual statements of truth, not determined or affected by feelings. You might *wish* the sky was green and the grass was blue, but that doesn't change reality.

Our culture *used to* recognize this difference between facts and feelings, and between truth and preference, understanding that in cases of provable reality the sentiment of "true for you, but not for me" doesn't work. However, modern culture for the most part, especially in matters of religion, morality, and identity, has moved away from the "objective" into the "subjective" when it comes to truth.

3. The abandonment of truth is wreaking havoc in the world.

The abandonment of truth is wreaking h_____ in the world.

We lost truth and God at the same time. Without one, we cannot have the other. They rise and fall together. If God does not define truth, then all humans are equal authorities and we can each define truth as we wish.

English writer Aldous Huxley said the reason he and his contemporaries were so eager to latch onto the theory of evolution was because belief in God was so restricting to their sexual preferences and evolution gave an explanation for reality that did not require God.

But this opens Pandora's box. Dostoyevsky, in his book *The Brothers Karamazov*, wrote, "If there is no God, all things are permissible." And, by implication, all truth is permissible. If we jettison God, we jettison truth or our claim to truth.

Do you believe the Holocaust was wrong? Why? Hitler thought it was right. Do you believe child pornography is wrong? Why? The pornographers think it is right. Do you think theft is wrong? Why? The thief thinks it is right. If you cannot appeal to an authority higher than humanity, you cannot say that something another person does is wrong. You and that other person are on the same moral level and cancel each other out. The best you can do is say that you do not prefer something. But you cannot call it wrong.

As a result, the world is a frightening place without God, without the Bible, and without truth. Attila the Hun, Genghis Khan, Nero, Hitler, Stalin, and a thousand nameless monsters throughout history are the legacy of mankind ruling others without God and the Bible. Right and wrong disappear, and those with the power make the rules.

And this is becoming a defining feature in today's world. During the 2012 presidential race, Harry Reid, the Democrat Senate majority leader, accused presidential candidate Mitt Romney from the floor of the Senate of having not paid any taxes over the past decade. Romney, in fact, had paid taxes and released his tax returns to prove it.

Fact checkers gave Reid the highest "bad mark rating" (four Pinocchios) for the claim. Everyone knew it was a lie. But Reid not only refused to retract the allegation, continuing to hammer on it, and seemed to almost take pride in the fact that it wasn't true. After the election, in an interview with a major news outlet, a reporter challenged Reid about continuing to defend the statement even though it was not true. His cold reply was, "Romney didn't win, did he?"

This is but a single sample of a reality that has taken hold in our post-truth world.

The collapse of biblical and traditional American values founded on Scripture is happening faster, and is going further, than anyone could possibly have imagined. As Christians fulfill their biblical responsibilities toward God, each other, and the lost world, we must stand on the foundation of truth. Not to do so casts us adrift on a sea of relativity in full sail. The high wind, driving our rudderless ship, blows us toward certain disaster.

4. When we reject God, we lose truth.

When we r_____ God, we lose truth.

How this disorienting state of affairs came about is tied to the fact that we, as a culture, have rejected God and His revealed truth. And without that touchpoint, each person is free to choose for himself what he will accept as truth and what he will not.

This has opened the door to a cultural shift unlike any in the history of the world. People used to accept that truth was external and feelings were internal. So, when our feelings conflicted with truth we aspired to bring our feelings into alignment with truth. Now, we aspire to bring truth into alignment with our feelings.

However, this shift has wreaked sudden and dramatic havoc on our American culture and on many other cultures around the world. Societal structure is breaking down because humanity cannot function in an orderly manner without truth. Life is reduced to the "survival of the fittest." Those in power inflict their values on those under power. The results are devastating.

5. Our challenge as Christians is to stand for truth as effectively as we can.

Our challenge as Christians is to s_____ for truth as effectively as we can.

We must stand against this cultural shift as best we can for three reasons:

- *First*, because not to do so is to fail at a fundamental Christian value.
- *Second*, because whatever affects our culture also affects the church. Christians are called to be "in" the world, but not "of" the world. Yet, noble as that sentiment is, we cannot deny that Christians are often compromised by culture, and to lose a cultural commitment to truth is to create another battlefront for Christians in their spiritual maturation process.
- *Third*, we are to be salt and light to the world around us. When we stand for truth, it leads others to truth and helps others, even non-Christians, have a better world.

There are also three things a Christian must do to combat this alarming cultural shift:

1. *We must not be fooled into getting soft on believing truth.* By "getting soft on truth," I mean getting deceived into accepting relativism and subjectivity regarding truth.

We must be defenders of God's truth revealed in Scripture, and champion the consistent and historical interpretation of Scripture. For two thousand years, the Bible has been clearly understood to teach principled living. Now, it is common for Christians to read rapidly changing and deteriorating cultural values back into Scripture and embrace interpretations that fly in the face of two thousand years of settled interpretation.

2. *We must not get deceived into not living the truth.* This, of course, rests on point #1. We normally live out that which we believe, but through ignorance Christians are getting deceived into living out truths that they have not adequately thought through. There are Christians who are not clear on the teachings of Scripture and who may condone unbiblical values, not realizing the Bible is actually clear on these subjects.

3. *We must not be intimidated into not speaking truth.* The most destructive influence of the politically correct cancel culture is to silence opposition. The majority of people in the United States do not agree with wildly unbiblical values, but they don't stand up for what they believe because they are fearful of losing their jobs or being thought of as intolerant or bigoted.

Conclusion

There are three things in our lives that we must keep in proper order: facts, faith, and feelings. All three must be alive and well if we are to live lives of purpose and satisfaction. But like the engine, coal car, and caboose of a train, they must be kept in the proper order. If you get them out of order, the train won't run.

Facts are the engine. They must be first. Truth must run our lives, not faith nor feelings. If unfounded, uninformed *faith* runs our lives, we may believe something that is wrong. If *feelings* run

206

our lives, we may do something that feels good upfront but hurts us down the road. Facts, and facts alone, can be trusted to lead our lives.

SO, DON'T SINK YOUR OWN SHIP.
TRUST FACTS TO GUIDE YOUR LIFE.

CHAPTER REVIEW

Repetition is the key to mental ownership.

Truth is true, no matter what you think, believe, or feel.

1. Truth is that which conforms to r_____.
2. Truth has become a choice between f_____ and f_____.
3. The abandonment of truth is wreaking h_____ in the world.
4. When we r_____ God, we lose truth.
5. Our challenge as Christians is to s_____ for truth as effectively as we can.

⛵ **DON'T SINK YOUR OWN SHIP**

If something is important, you must repeat it until it changes you.

Chapter Summaries

1. Look to God for h_____.
2. R_____ q_____ when you sin.
3. Be totally o_____ to God.
4. Be a good s_____ of life's resources.
5. Be a s_____ to others.
6. Choose the f_____ of self-discipline.
7. Don't let m_____ become m_____.
8. G_____ your mind to g_____ your life.
9. Use your tongue to h_____, not to h_____.
10. Trust God's definition of s_____.
11. Keep your c_____ clear.
12. Nurture your r_____.
13. Pay the p_____ to be patient.
14. Accept that without p_____ there is no g_____.

15. Renew your m_____ to transform your l_____.
16. Don't play c_____ while God is playing c_____.
17. Trust f_____ to guide your life.

 LIFE-CHECK

Answer these questions, either individually by journaling the answer or in a spiritual accountability group.

1. What experience have you had in which you denied reality, persisted in foolishness, and paid a significant price?
2. Did you learn your lesson, or are you still struggling in that area?
3. Do you agree that absolute truth exists and that the Bible is totally true? If not, how do you determine what is true and what isn't?
4. If truth sets us free, what is an area of your life in which truth has set you free?

 FOR FURTHER REFLECTION

Additional Scripture.

Joshua 1:8	John 8:32
Judges 21:25	John 17:17
Psalm 119:9, 11	2 Timothy 2:15

 RESOURCES

For further study.

Relativism: Feet Firmly Planted in Mid-Air, Greg Koukl

What You Need to Know about the Bible, Max Anders

CHAPTER 18

TRUST GOD AND OBEY HIM

DON'T SINK YOUR OWN SHIP.
TRUST GOD AND OBEY HIM.

Faith is only as good as the object in which it is placed.

Now faith is the certainty of things hoped for, a proof of things not seen.

—HEBREWS 11:1

James Herriot is the pen name of a veterinarian who wrote a series of books about his life in the Yorkshire highlands of northern England. He had more than his share of unusual and even dangerous things happen to him during his life, some of them due strictly to chance and others brought on by some of his own glaring lapses in judgment.

One such lapse came when Herriot was making his rounds in the hilly high country near his home, driving a car with bad brakes. As he neared a precipitous hill with dangerous curves in the road, he couldn't decide whether or not to chance driving down it. It was much shorter to go down the steep hill with four menacing turns, but it was a little dangerous because of his bad brakes. To turn around and go the long way was much safer, but it meant a round trip of nearly ten miles. The place he needed to go was just at the bottom of the hill. He could see it from the top.

Finally, after much deliberation, Herriot decided to place his faith in the bad brakes. Over the hill he went, dry-mouthed and white-knuckled. The whole world seemed to drop away from him, and the road felt nearly vertical. From there, I'll let him tell the story:

It is surprising what speed you can attain in bottom gear if you have nothing else to hold you back and as the first bend rushed up at me the little engine started a rising scream of protest. When I hit the curve, I hauled the wheel round desperately to the right, the tyres spun for a second in the stones and loose soil of the verge, then we were off again.

This was a longer stretch and even steeper and it was like being on [a roller coaster] with the same feeling of lack of control over one's fate. Hurtling into the bend, the idea of turning at this speed was preposterous but it was that or straight over the edge. Terror-stricken, I closed my eyes and dragged the wheel to the left. [I was sure the car would turn over, but it didn't,] and I was once more on my way.

Again a yawning gradient. But as the car sped downwards, engine howling, I was aware of a curious numbness. I seemed to have reached the ultimate limits of fear and hardly noticed as we shot round the third bend. One more to go and at last the road was leveling out; my speed dropped rapidly and at the last bend I couldn't have been doing more than twenty. I had made it.

It wasn't till I was right on to the final straight that I saw the sheep. Hundreds of them, filling the road. A river of woolly backs lapping from wall to wall. They were only yards from me and I was still going downhill. Without hesitation I turned and drove straight into the wall. . . .

I suppose some people would have asked me what [I was

doing], but not a Dales shepherd. He went quietly by without invading my privacy, but when I looked in the mirror after a few moments I could see him in the middle of the road staring back at me, his sheep temporarily forgotten.[1]

I have laughed at that story until I thought I would injure myself, probably because in smaller, less wacky ways I have done exactly the same thing. *Blind* faith is not only futile, but it can be downright dangerous. Faith is only as safe as the thing in which it is placed. James Herriot put his faith in bad brakes, and it almost cost him his life.

God wants Christians to have peace, love, and joy in life, but in order for this to happen we must believe the right things. We must trust the promises of God. That's why faith cannot lead our lives. Facts must. Once we get our facts straight, we then know where to put our faith.

This is a crucial thing to understand. We do what we do because we *believe* it will make us happy. We may be dead wrong, and often are, but we do it nevertheless because of what we believe. When a Christian deliberately and knowingly sins, it is a breakdown of faith. He believes that the sin will make him happier than God will. The opposite of obedience, then, is not disobedience. *The opposite of obedience is unbelief!*

If we believe/trust God, we obey Him. If we do not obey Him, it is because we do not believe/trust Him.

Therefore, it is vital for us to be alert to what we believe and, as I said earlier, be sure that what we believe is rooted in facts/truth/reality.

1. Faith is believing what God has said and acting accordingly.

Faith is believing what God has said and a_____ accordingly.

Some cynics have defined faith as "believing in spite of the fact that there is nothing to believe." Or, worse, "believing in spite of all the evidence to the contrary." Mark Twain famously said, "Faith is believing in something you just know ain't true."

In the classic movie *Miracle on 34th Street*, Santa Claus utters what much of the world thinks faith is: "Faith is believing in things when common sense tells you not to."

Going down a slightly different path, in the vintage cartoon *Pinocchio* Jiminy Cricket sings, "When you wish upon a star, your dreams come true." That's what faith is like for many people—wishful thinking. Jiminy believes that if you wish hard enough, your dreams will come true. Many people think that if they just believe hard enough, their prayers will come true. But that simply isn't true. Faith in *faith* is no good. Believing is futile if you are believing something that isn't true.

Let me offer a better definition of faith: Faith is believing *what God has revealed* and *acting accordingly*.

When we do that, we are on safe ground. Our degree of obedience to God and the Scriptures is the manifestation of the degree of our faith. It must be facts first, faith second.

2. If we believe, we obey.

If we believe, we o_____.

If we don't want our life going off the rails, we must keep *facts, faith, and feelings* in their proper order. Facts are the engine of life. And facts are what give us an object worthy of our faith.

When it comes to faith, many of us are like the man you've likely heard of who was walking along a narrow path paying little attention to where he was going. Suddenly he slipped over the edge of a cliff. As he fell, he grabbed a branch growing from the side of the cliff. Realizing that he couldn't hang on for long, he yelled, "Help! Is anybody up there?"

A great, booming voice answered, "Yes, I'm here."

"Who's that?" the man asked.

"I'm your guardian angel," the great booming voice replied.

"Help me!"

"Do you trust me?"

"Yes, I trust you completely!"

"Then let go of the branch," the angel said.

"What?!"

"Let go of the branch."

There was a long pause. Finally, the man yelled, "Is there anybody else up there?"

When we get into life's scrapes, when we flounder for direction, when we ache for consolation, when we yearn for fellowship, when we are desperate for deliverance, we cry out to God for help. But, then, when the Lord makes it clear what we are to do, we often wonder if there is *"anybody else up there"*!

In spite of the fact that God's way is not necessarily easy, it is always the best way. The more completely we believe this, the better our lives will go and the more our lives will be a testimony to the grace and sufficiency of the Lord. The *fact* is, the shortest distance between us and the life we long for is total obedience to Christ, and we need to place our faith in that fact.

3. We can take practical steps to increase our faith.

We can take practical steps to i_____ our faith.

How can we increase our faith? I read one time of a good example. A suspension bridge was planned to span a wide gorge out west. Everything about the construction of the bridge seemed fairly straightforward except how to get started.

Finally, someone came up with an ingenious strategy. The builders shot an arrow from one side of the gorge to the other. The arrow carried a tiny thread across the gulf. The thread was used to pull a piece of twine across, the twine pulled after it a small rope, the rope soon carried a cable across, and in time came the iron chains that the bridge was to hang from.

This is much like faith or any number of things in life that need to be strengthened. We start with where we are and grow from there. Although often weak in its beginning stages, a seemingly small faith can draw us to a stronger and stronger faith that will be used by God in greater and greater ways.

The beginning point . . . the arrow shooting the first thread over the gorge . . . is to accept that God is all-knowing, all-powerful, everywhere simultaneously, and all-good. Therefore, He is worthy of being trusted.

Next, the twine that follows is that if we trust God, we obey Him, and if we do not obey Him, it is because we do not trust Him. So, we must tie our obedience to our faith and choose to trust in the One whom we believe to be trustworthy. The opposite of obedience is not disobedience. The opposite of obedience is unbelief. If we need to be more disciplined in our Christian life, we focus on faith, not self-discipline.

The rope that follows is to fill our minds with the Scriptures that teach and verify the wisdom of trusting and obeying. James 1:2–4 says, "Consider it all joy, my brothers and sisters, when you encounter various trials, knowing that the testing of your faith produces endurance. And let endurance have its perfect result, so that you may be perfect and complete, lacking in nothing."

Trials are like spiritual exercise machines that God uses to make us spiritually fit. So, we trust that fact, we trust God in the hard times of life, and we strive to be obedient to all we understand He is asking of us.

We tie our study of Scripture to our decision to trust the One we have accepted as trustworthy. We accept that the trials God brings into our lives are the very means He uses to make us spiritually strong. In order to glean insight into our own lives, we study passages that make the link between faith and obedience and we observe examples of faithful obedience in Scripture.

Next, the cable we pull across the gorge is to memorize and mentally rehearse key "faith" and "obedience" passages in order to burn their truth deeply into our minds and hearts.

Finally, the chain that holds the "bridge" of faith is prayer and communion with God, although asking the Lord to increase and strengthen our faith is actually a part of all the levels of faith. In a powerful prayer in Psalm 139:23–24, we read, "Search me, God, and know my heart; put me to the test and know my anxious thoughts; and see if there is any hurtful way in me, and lead me in the everlasting way."

It is a mark of the normal Christian life that no matter where we are in our walk with the Lord, we will likely feel that our faith is weak and in need of strengthening. This prayer opens us to a deep work of God as He brings into our lives all that we need to strengthen our faith.

So, this is not a hard and fast analogy, but in general it helps us understand a process we can use to *cooperate* with God in the pursuit of greater biblical faith. As we look to the Lord and His Word, and as we pray to Him to work in our hearts, we strengthen each step of the process and pursue an increasingly mature relationship with Him.

Beyond these overarching principles, here are some obvious practical ways we can begin to build our faith:

- Be faithful to the spiritual disciplines of reading the Bible, studying it, memorizing and meditating on it, praying, going to church, integrating your life with other Christians, etc.
- Read books and/or search the internet to read/watch stories of people who have exercised strong faith in obedience to the truths of Scripture.
- Join or create a spiritual accountability group that focuses on this authentic pursuit of the Lord.
- Get involved in sharing your faith and exercising your gifts and talents, which can be a significant faith-builder.
- Financially support valuable ministries to help them fulfill their vision.

Conclusion

God's way is always the best way. The more completely we believe this, the better our lives will go and the more our lives will be a testimony to the grace and sufficiency of the Lord.

The *fact* is, the shortest distance between us and the life we long for is total obedience to Christ. As we believe that and obey that reality, our faith strengthens and grows and transforms us more and more into the character image of Christ.

So, don't sink your own ship.
Trust God and obey Him.

CHAPTER REVIEW

Repetition is the key to mental ownership.

Faith is only as good as the object in which it is placed.

1. Faith is believing what God has said and a_____ accordingly.
2. If we believe, we o_____.
3. We can take practical steps to i_____ our faith.

DON'T SINK YOUR OWN SHIP

If something is important, you must repeat it until it changes you.

Chapter Summaries

1. Look to God for h_____.
2. R_____ q_____ when you sin.
3. Be totally o_____ to God.
4. Be a good s_____ of life's resources.
5. Be a s_____ to others.
6. Choose the f_____ of self-discipline.
7. Don't let m_____ become m_____.
8. G_____ your mind to g_____ your life.
9. Use your tongue to h_____, not to h_____.
10. Trust God's definition of s_____.
11. Keep your c_____ clear.
12. Nurture your r_____.
13. Pay the p_____ to be patient.
14. Accept that without p_____ there is no g_____.
15. R_____ your mind to t_____ your life.
16. Don't play c_____ while God is playing c____.
17. Trust f_____ to guide your life.
18. Trust God and o_____ Him.

LIFE-CHECK

Answer these questions, either individually by journaling the answer or in a spiritual accountability group.

1. How would you have defined faith before you read this chapter? Have you ever been misled in your understanding of the Christian life by a false understanding of faith?
2. In the list of "obvious practical ways" to build your faith listed earlier, in which item do you feel the strongest? In which do you feel the weakest?
3. What specific steps do you think you can take to strengthen your faith?
4. Evaluate how fully you think you believe this statement: "Everything God asks of us is to give something good to us and keep some harm from us; therefore, the shortest distance between you and the life you long for is total obedience to Christ."

 FOR FURTHER REFLECTION

Additional Scripture.

Luke 17:5–6   Hebrews 11:1, 6
Romans 12:1–2   Jude 3, 20
1 Corinthians 16:13

 RESOURCES

For further study.

Trusting God, Jerry Bridges
30 Days to Growing in Your Faith (Chapter 18), Max Anders

CHAPTER 19

DON'T LEAD WITH YOUR EMOTIONS

Don't sink your own ship.
Don't lead with your emotions.

Feelings must follow facts and faith, not lead them.

Like a city that is broken into and without walls
So is a person who has no self-control over his spirit.
—PROVERBS 25:28

High school football is wildly popular in Texas. I heard a story one time of an oil tycoon from West Texas many years ago, who was desperate for a victory by his local team. He promised each player and coach a free car if they would defeat their bitter rivals in the next game.

The team went crazy with anticipation. They jumped and hollered in delirium as they each envisioned themselves in their new car. For the next seven days, the boys ate, drank, and breathed football, fortified to before-unknown heights of enthusiasm with continuous fantasies of new cars and the exalted life they would bring.

Finally, the big night arrived and the team assembled in their locker room. Excitement was at an unprecedented high. The coach made several inane comments and the boys hurried out to face the enemy. They assembled on the sidelines, put their hands together, and shouted a simultaneous "Rah!" Then they ran onto the field and were demolished, thirty-eight to zero.

The team's exuberance didn't translate into a single point on the scoreboard. Seven days of unbridled enthusiasm simply couldn't compensate for the difference in talent, discipline, and coaching.

Such is the nature of emotions. They don't make a good engine—they only make a good caboose.

Leading with your emotions is like a boxer leading with his chin. It's only a matter of time until he gets decked. However, leading with emotions is Standard Operating Procedure today. People gush about "following their heart" and "just wanting to be happy." Then they don't understand why they are always getting knocked face-down on the canvas of life.

The reality is, *truth is what God says it is*, regardless of what we believe, regardless of how much faith we have in our beliefs, and *regardless of how we feel.*

Feelings or emotions aren't bad. In the Bible, we see that God has emotions. That's why we have emotions—we are created in His image. God experiences joy, sorrow, peace, compassion, and anger. As a result, so do we. We are emotional beings, and that isn't bad.

But emotions can also be a reflection of decisions we've made, or truth we believe, or values we possess. If we've made bad decisions, or believed a lie(s), or possess faulty values, our emotions can spiral downward in God's severe mercy to alert us to our need to correct bad decisions, wrong beliefs, or faulty values.

So, how do we live with our emotions? We must understand them, know their place in the Christian life, and know when to trust them and when not to trust them.

1. God uses positive emotions to enrich our lives.

God uses positive emotions to e_____ our lives.

Emotions can obviously enrich our lives when things are going well. When we receive a promotion or earn a reward or go through a positive life transition, deeply rewarding emotions can significantly enrich our lives.

When we live a life of faithful obedience to God, a life of trust in Him, and a life of love, compassion, and forgiveness toward others, we *feel* enriched and blessed. We experience the fruit of the Spirit, which are love, joy, and peace.

This is especially important when circumstances are difficult, exemplified when the apostle Paul was imprisoned with his friend and fellow laborer, Silas. Before being jailed they were arrested, taken before the city officials, and beaten with rods. The Bible says: "When they had struck them with many blows, they threw them into prison, commanding the jailer to guard them securely; and he, having received such a command, threw them into the inner prison and fastened their feet in the stocks. Now about midnight Paul and Silas were praying and singing hymns of praise to God" (Acts 16:23–25).

Paul and Silas had been arrested, humiliated, beaten, and imprisoned, yet they prayed and sang hymns of praise afterward. That is what can happen when one lives in deep trust and obedience with the Lord.

Paul is the same person who was beaten many times, shipwrecked, attacked by animals, stoned, and left for dead, yet said that "our momentary, light affliction is producing for us an eternal weight of glory far beyond all comparison" (2 Cor. 4:17). The Lord can give us positive emotions even in the midst of the most difficult of circumstances, which make such experiences much easier to deal with.

2. God uses negative emotions to warn us of a need to change something.

God uses negative emotions to warn us of a need to c_____ something.

Negative emotions such as unresolved anger, depression, and anxiety can warn us that our life is out of balance and we need to change something. When David was at the height of his power he committed adultery with Bathsheba, the wife of one of his greatest generals. Then, to cover up the adultery, he had the general killed. It was a ghastly abuse of power, which he likely would have gotten away with if it were only a matter of his brute power as king. But the eyes of God saw it all, and David fell under deep conviction by the Holy Spirit. He writes of that experience in Psalm 32:3–5:

> When I kept silent about my sin, my body wasted away
> Through my groaning all day long.
> For day and night Your hand was heavy upon me;
> My vitality failed as with the dry heat of summer.
> I acknowledged my sin to You,
> And I did not hide my guilt.
> I said, "I will confess my wrongdoings to the LORD";
> And You forgave the guilt of my sin.

When we sin, God convicts us of that sin (John 16:8), and the terrible negative emotions we feel are intended to get us to repent and change our behavior. In 2 Corinthians 7:10 the apostle Paul acknowledges, "the sorrow that is according to the will of God produces a repentance without regret."

Negative emotions *can* be the result of physical problems. Maybe we are ill, or our blood chemistry is out of balance, or medication we're taking has us emotionally off balance. Perhaps we are working too hard, not getting enough rest, or eating poorly. These issues should all be addressed. *However,* when negative emotions are the result of spiritual issues God can use them to lead us to Scripture, prayer, wise counsel, repentance, and anything else He might lead us to, in order that we can grow and be strengthened in our spiritual walk.

In short, there are times when we must not do something our emotions are telling us to do.

So, we've seen that emotions in and of themselves are not bad, but we do need to understand them. They can be good. They can deeply enrich our lives. But, on the other hand, unguided and unguarded emotions can lead us astray and turn our emotional experiences into pain instead of pleasure. We've also seen that God uses *negative* emotions to convict us and guide us into correct and joyful living.

3. The will of God can be frightening.

The will of God can be f_____.

Walking off a cliff backward can teach you a lot about yourself. To be honest, the first time this happened to me I didn't actually *walk*; it was more like a crawl . . . a shinny, actually. I was teaching at a college in Phoenix, Arizona, and one day several of my students approached me. "Mr. Anders," they said, "we are going up on Squaw Peak to do a little rappelling off some of the cliffs on Saturday. Would you like to go?"

It was hard for me to say no. For one thing, I didn't want to appear chicken. Then, never having been rappelling before, I didn't understand how truly terrifying it would be. So, stifling every instinct to the contrary, I nonchalantly said, "Sure."

When we got to the mountain the next Saturday, I'll never forget walking over to the edge of a cliff and looking down for the first time—the cliff was the height of a ten-story building!

They explained to me that the rope, which was the diameter of my thumb, was rated to hold twelve hundred pounds.

Uh-huh.

So they clipped me into a webbed, diaper-like contraption made out of seat belt material, threaded the rope through a big paper clip attached to my diaper, and said, "Just lean back against the rope and walk backward off the cliff."

Right!

I didn't trust the rope. As a kid back in Indiana, we used to swing on ropes in the barn that were as big around as my wrist. Those would hold a guy. This little thing *might* hold—it might *not*. And the big paper clip (i.e., carabiner) that held me in my seat belt diaper and attached me to the rope—well, it didn't look strong enough to hold a Thanksgiving turkey! I didn't have faith in my equipment, and I was terrified.

But there I was—halfway over the edge. I was too proud to climb back up, but too scared to lean back and walk down. So I began to sort of shinny down, holding the rope so tightly that I didn't even need any other equipment. With my legs wrapped around the rope, hunched over in a modified fetal position, I squirmed down over the edge. It was not a pretty sight.

Before I had gotten a third of the way down, my arms were trembling and almost useless. My kneecaps were sore from bumping against the face of the cliff, while my hands and elbows were bruised and aching. I hung there, swinging gently like a ham in a smokehouse, lips and cheek pressed against the face of the cliff, wondering if I would ever see another sunrise.

With infinite patience, the leader of the group yelled down, "Lean back, Mr. Anders."

In utter contradiction to reality, I yelled up, "I am leaning back!"

Finally, with exhaustion eroding my will to live, I concluded that I would never get out of there alive anyway if I didn't do something, so I did what he said. I leaned back against the rope until my feet were flat against the face of the cliff. Then I let the rope slip through the carabiner, and . . . I scaled effortlessly down the face of the cliff!

Once down, I rushed back up to go again.

I learned that day that you have to trust your rope when rappelling. You have to believe that it will hold you and act accordingly. If you trust in your own strength to get you down, this will sap every ounce of energy before you even get close to the ground and leave you hanging helplessly in space.

When it comes to the spiritual life, we are like rappelers. The cliff is life. The rope is God. If we try to make it over the cliff in our own strength and enough things go wrong (and they will), this will sap the life out of us. But if we lean back on the rope, believing that God will hold us, we will make it down the cliff of life.

As I mentioned earlier in this chapter, there are times when emotions tell you to do something and you shouldn't. Leading with our emotions through the maze of life can lead us to predictable bad decisions.

But there are other times when your emotions will tell you *not* to do something and you should. That's what we want to look at now.

There are times when the will of God can seem as terrifying as walking over to a cliff and looking down. Every instinct in you screams to back up and walk away.

Take Jesus as an example. On the night in which He was to be betrayed by Judas, He went to the garden of Gethsemane with His disciples to pray and prepare for the unspeakable horror of the coming hours, when He would suffer and die. In spite of the fact that He was God and knew He would be resurrected, He was, nevertheless, still also a man and the terror of the coming events overwhelmed Him.

Jesus said to His disciples, "My soul is exceedingly sorrowful, even to death" (Matthew 26:38). He had done nothing wrong, yet He was engulfed in grief. The will of God was terrifying.

Yet Jesus trusted His Heavenly Father. Because He trusted Him, He obeyed Him. And though it was unimaginably difficult, God's grace sustained Him. In the end, all was well.

We live in a fallen world, and even when we believe the right things and make good decisions, we are not exempt from the possibility of great emotional upheaval. Living in fellowship and obedience to God doesn't always lessen the pain we go through, but it makes it possible to bear.

Sometimes God's will asks us to make a decision that is frightening. If we have wronged someone, the will of God may require us to go back to that person, ask for forgiveness, and possibly offer restitution. That can be very scary, yet it is clear that God is asking us to do it. So we make a difficult decision and, trusting God, we obey.

Our vocation may require us to do things that violate our standards as a believer and God may ask us to change vocations. The uncertainty, and perhaps the reality that this will result in our making less money, can be deeply unnerving. Yet God is asking this of us. So, we are to make the difficult decision to trust God and obey.

Or, we are not being asked by God to make a decision, to do or not do something, but a *circumstance* comes upon us. We lose our job. We learn that we have a serious illness. Someone we deeply love dies. Circumstances, that God has allowed, are suddenly terrifying.

Through it all, our model is Jesus. In addition to the example of Gethsemane we looked at earlier, listen to Hebrews 12:1–3:

> Let's rid ourselves of every obstacle and the sin which so easily entangles us, and let's run with endurance the race that is set before us, looking only at Jesus, the originator and perfecter of the faith, who for the joy set before Him endured the cross, despising the shame, and has sat down at the right hand of the throne of God.
>
> For consider Him who has endured such hostility by sinners against Himself, so that you will not grow weary and lose heart.

During the times of life when God's will is as terrifying as looking down a cliff, we choose to follow the truth rather than our emotions. At those times, we need to take stock of reality:

- God is all-good and all-powerful.
- God loves us.
- God's will is best for us.
- God will never lead us where His grace cannot sustain us.
- Every loss we accept on earth is disproportionately rewarded in heaven.
- In the end, all will be well.

Said more succinctly, the Rope will hold us.

So, we choose to "go over the cliff" regardless of what our emotions are telling us, believing that the Rope will hold us.

4. Emotions must be kept in check if we are to make good decisions.

Emotions must be kept in check if we are to make g_____ decisions.

Whether they are telling us to do something we ought not, or telling us not to do something we ought, emotions must be kept in check if we are to make good decisions.

I remember the time I wanted some bongo drums. I was walking past a music store with my mother and brother and saw a pair of bongo drums in the window, and something deep within me cried out to own those drums. My desire grew like a fire in a dry house, and before long my whole life was consumed with getting those drums. I was about thirteen or fourteen years old and had worked at odd jobs long enough to be able to plunk down the rather sizable sum of thirty dollars for them.

Almost the instant I bought the drums, I knew I had made a mistake. What can you do with bongo drums? I didn't play with a calypso band. I didn't play with *any* band. I took the drums home, and by the time I had whacked around on them for thirty minutes, I had exhausted what you can do alone with bongo drums. I put them down and stared at them. Resentment started to build. I began to visualize all the other things I could have bought with that money that would have been fun for a long time. The drums sat around our house unplayed for the next ten years until the drum heads split from old age and my mother got rid of them.

This was a painful but profitable lesson, and it has saved me from many subsequent bad decisions. Whenever I feel an irrational desire for something rise up and grab me by the throat, I can scoff at the desire and say, "You're nothing but a set of bongo drums in disguise."

Make no mistake, it's hard to make the right decisions when we're emotionally involved. But the question is, how much do we want to suffer? Would we rather experience the short-term pain of right decisions, or the long-term pain of wrong decisions? Less pain comes from right decisions.

God has put faith at the center of the Christian life in three steps:

- Reveal truth: God revealed His truth to humanity. In the earliest days, He did this directly through prophets, dreams, visions, or direct contact. However, He also oversaw the writing down of His revelation so that His primary means of revelation today is the Bible (Hebrews 4:12).
- Require faith: Many of the things that God asks of us in His revelation take us 180 degrees in the opposite direction of our natural inclinations. Therefore, we will only respond appropriately if we believe God and trust His word. When we trust, we obey (John 14:15). When we do not obey, it is because we do not trust.

- Reward obedience: We reap the consequences of our faith. If we follow God in faithful and trusting obedience, He rewards us (Psalm 19:11). If we do not, He chastens us (Hebrews 12:4–11).

God's desire is to nurture our faith by rewarding us for obedience, strengthening our faith, and increasing our readiness to obey.

Conclusion

We see that not feelings but faith, based on facts, is the heart of the Christian life. All God wants from us is to believe in Him and trust Him, demonstrated by doing as He says.

- "Without faith it is impossible to please Him, for the one who comes to God must believe that He exists, and that He proves to be One who rewards those who seek Him" (Hebrews 11:6).
- "The righteous One will live by faith" (Romans 1:17).
- "We walk by faith, not by sight" (2 Corinthians 5:7).

So, just as a rappeler must trust the rope, the Christian must trust God and trust His Word, believing that as we exercise faith God will demonstrate His truth to be reliable.

SO, DON'T SINK YOUR OWN SHIP.
DON'T LEAD WITH YOUR EMOTIONS.

CHAPTER REVIEW

Repetition is the key to mental ownership.

Feelings must follow facts and faith, not lead them.

1. God uses positive emotions to e_____ our lives.
2. God uses negative emotions to warn us of a need to c_____ something.
3. The will of God can be f_____.
4. Emotions must be kept in check if we are to make g_____ decisions.

DON'T SINK YOUR OWN SHIP

If something is important, you must repeat it until it changes you.

Chapter Summaries

1. Look to God for h_____.
2. R_____ q_____ when you sin.
3. Be totally o_____ to God.
4. Be a good s_____ of life's resources.
5. Be a s_____ to others.
6. Choose the f_____ of self-discipline.
7. Don't let m_____ become m_____.
8. G_____ your mind to g_____ your life.
9. Use your tongue to h_____, not to h_____.
10. Trust God's definition of s_____.
11. Keep your c_____ clear.
12. Nurture your r_____.
13. Pay the p_____ to be patient.
14. Accept that without p_____ there is no g_____.
15. R_____ your mind to t_____ your life.
16. Don't play c_____ while God is playing c_____.

17. Trust f_____ to guide your life.

18. Trust God and o_____ Him.

19. Don't l____ with your emotions.

 LIFE-CHECK

Answer these questions, either individually by journaling the answer or in a spiritual accountability group.

1. Describe times in your life when you have experienced particularly positive emotions. How did God use them to enrich your life?

2. Describe times in your life when you have experienced particularly negative emotions. What was God trying to warn you of? Do you have any insight on what you might have done to bring these emotions on yourself?

3. Describe times in your life when you have experienced emotional pain due to circumstances beyond your control (death of a loved one, physical illness, etc.). What truth about life was reinforced through that experience?

 FOR FURTHER REFLECTION

Additional Scripture.

Proverbs 25:28

Acts 16:23–25

1 Corinthians 13:4–7

2 Corinthians 4:16–18

2 Corinthians 7:10

Galatians 5:22–23

Philippians 4:8–9

 RESOURCES

For further study.

Emotions: Can You Trust Them?, James Dobson

30 Days to Growing in Your Faith (Chapters 6, 19, 28), Max Anders

CHAPTER 20

DON'T JUST SIT THERE, DO SOMETHING

DON'T SINK YOUR OWN SHIP.
DON'T JUST SIT THERE, DO SOMETHING.

To be free to sail the seven seas, you must make yourself a
slave to the compass.

Be on the alert, stand firm in the faith, act like men, be strong.
—1 CORINTHIANS 16:13

I said in the introduction that this is not a deep book. I didn't
intend it to be.

But I did intend to give you a basic overview of some of the
important issues in living the Christian life, and to whet your appe-
tite for the possibility that you might be able to make progress in
some important areas faster and easier than you may have thought.

In contrast to this, the book may also have revealed some areas
in which you need or want to go a little deeper, in which case there
are life-check questions, additional Scriptures, and resources for
further study.

Having said all this, I want to make four other points about the
spiritual growth process.

1. Everything you learn today is based on what you learned yesterday.

Everything you learn t_____ is based on what you learned y_____.

And what you can learn tomorrow is based on what you learned today. So, when building a mature knowledge of a subject, it is important to have a solid foundation on which to build. Otherwise, you may find yourself trying to build a mature knowledge of something without having even mastered the very basics of the subject.

The old saying is that the size of the building you can build is determined by the size of your foundation.

This being the case, it is essential for the Christian life to have a complete foundation on which to build. If you have never gained such a foundation, I would encourage you to read two books which are designed to do just that:

a. *30 Days to Understanding the Bible*

This book is designed to give you a basic knowledge of the facts of the Bible (people, places, events in chronological order) and the teachings of the Bible (what the Bible says about God, Christ, the Holy Spirit, sin, salvation, the church, future things, etc.). This book will lay a very basic foundation of that information faster and easier than any other resource.

b. *30 Days to Growing in Your Faith*

This book is designed to give you a basic knowledge of the principles of Christian living (what does the Bible say about how to pray, how to discern God's will, how to walk in the Spirit, etc.). It contains the information that I desperately wish I had been given many years ago when I first became a Christian. It would've made such a difference then.

These two books are not the most you will need to know; they are the least. They are not the end of the knowledge we need; they are the beginning. They do not provide the superstructure of your Christian life; they provide the foundation.

Whether you are a newer Christian or whether you have been a Christian for some time, these books are likely to give you helpful information which you did not have before. They also can give you the big picture so that it is easier for you to understand the details of the Christian life.

2. Knowledge isn't everything, but everything rests on knowledge.

Knowledge isn't everything, but everything r_____ on knowledge.

- You cannot believe something until you know it.
- You will not live it until you believe it.
- You will not be happy until you live it.

So, no, knowledge isn't everything, but everything rests on knowledge. Thus, it is vital for you to gain a progressive understanding of the Christian faith and how to live.

Having said this, it is equally vital to go beyond knowledge to life change. Ultimately, the Christian life is measured not by what we know but by who we are. It is not knowledge, but character based on knowledge that must be our driving motivation.

3. Mental renewal is essential to a transformed life.

Mental r_____ is essential to a t_____ life.

As we saw in chapter 15 of this book, Romans 12:2 teaches that we can be living demonstrations of the fact that God's will is good and perfect and acceptable, but only if we are transformed. And we will only be transformed as our mind is renewed. So, again, mental renewal is essential to a transformed life.

Also, repetition is the key to mental renewal. If something is important, we must repeat it until it changes us. Repetition rewires the brain, altering our fundamental attitudes, values, and behavior and changing us from the inside out. That is why the Bible makes such a strong case for mastering and meditating on Scripture (Psalm 1; Joshua 1:8).

To that end, an additional resource that can make a powerful contribution to your spiritual life is the Change Zone (thechange-zone.com). It is designed to guide you through Scripture passages, biblical affirmations, and powerful spiritual insights each day, filling your mind with truth that will "set you free" (John 8:32). I encourage you to enroll today.

4. We can use neuroscience to guide our daily walk with God.

We can use neuroscience to g_____ our daily walk with God.

The following is a list of things that the Bible tells us to do. Neuroscience sheds light on why and how. I have included quotes from Dr. Caroline Leaf's book *Switch On Your Brain* to amplify the importance of these disciplines.

a. **Make a commitment to daily time with God (Deuteronomy 6:4–7)**
   - "Self-directed neuroplasticity is a general description of the principle that deep thinking changes brain structure and function" (p. 130).
   - "You can change your brain with your mind and essentially renew your mind" (p. 25).
   - "As we consciously direct our thinking, we can wire out toxic patterns of thinking and replace them with healthy thoughts. New thought networks grow. We increase our intelligence and bring healing to our brains, minds, and physical bodies." (p. 20).

b. **Make Scripture the core of your daily time with God (Joshua 1:8)**
   o "The primary success of capturing your thoughts will be to focus on God's way first, not the world's ways. And science is showing that meditating on the elements of Jesus' teachings rewires healthy new circuits in the brain" (p. 73).
   o "When we pray, when we catch our thoughts, when we memorize and quote Scripture, we move into [a] deep meditative state" (p. 84).

c. **Include prayer and meditation (Psalm 1)**
   o "When we direct our rest by introspection, self-reflection, and prayer; when we catch our thoughts; when we memorize and quote Scripture; when we develop our mind intellectually, we . . . improve brain function as well as mind, body, and spiritual health" (p. 91).
   o "Regular meditators—by this I mean those who have adopted a disciplined and focused, reflecting thought life in which they bring all their thoughts into captivity—[have a brain which is] more active, growing more branches and integrating and linking thoughts, which translates as increased intelligence and wisdom and that wonderful feeling of peace. God also throws in some additional benefits such as increased immune and cardiovascular health." (p. 84).

d. **Guard your brain (2 Corinthians 10:5)**
   o "The subconscious . . . mind is filled with the thoughts you have been building since you were in the womb, and they form the perceptual base from which you see life. Up to 99% of the decisions you make are based on what you have [built into your nonconscious mind]. If a person's nonconscious . . . mind is filled with negative, toxic trash, then that is what informs his or her decisions on a day-to-day basis, which means that a person will speak and act from that toxicity" (p. 133).

- "The brain, far from being fixed in toxicity, can change even in the most challenging neurological situations" (p. 20).

e. **Nurture a plan to develop your mind intellectually (2 Peter 3:18)**

- "Each morning when you wake up, you have new baby nerve cells inside your brain to use wisely as you remove bad thoughts and wire in new ones" (pp. 25–26).

- "As we think, we change the physical nature of our brain. As we consciously direct our thinking, we can wire out toxic patterns of thinking and replace them with healthy thoughts. New thought networks grow. We increase our intelligence and bring healing to our brains, minds, and physical bodies" (p. 20).

f. **Feed your subconscious, and then wait for your subconscious to feed you (Proverbs 2:1–12)**

- "What you wire into your brain through thinking is stored in your nonconscious mind. The nonconscious mind is where 99.9% of our mind activity is. It is the root level that stores the thoughts with the emotions and perceptions, and it impacts the conscious mind and what we say and do" (p. 123).

- "Whatever you think about the most will grow . . . you can't just apply a thought once and think change has happened. It takes repeated work . . ." (p. 128).

Conclusion

This is not a complete list of spiritual disciplines. It's just a list of obvious implications of neuroscience to a Christian's daily life, and these are all things the Bible has already told us to do. Neuroscience just gives us additional information as to why and how.

As Dr. Leaf said, "God was so serious about us capturing our thoughts and renewing our minds that He gave us science as an encouragement."

One additional factor that is important for us to remember is that *the Holy Spirit guides and empowers this whole process.* It is true that mental renewal processes work for non-Christians, but for Christians the Holy Spirit and the Scriptures bring a divine presence and power that are not there for the non-Christian:

- The Holy Spirit convicts us of sin and calls us to righteousness (John 16:8).
- The Holy Spirit illumines our minds to understand the truth of Scripture (1 Corinthians 2:10–16).
- The Holy Spirit guides and strengthens us to live as we ought (Ephesians 3:16)
- The Holy Spirit leads us (Romans 8:14).
- The Holy Spirit takes the mental renewal process (Romans 12:2) to a whole new level not available to non-Christians. We must have the Holy Spirit's direct involvement in this process for it to fully work for Christians as God intended.

In everything God asks of us, He does so to give something good to us and keep some harm from us. Therefore, the shortest distance between us and the life we long for is total obedience to Christ. Throwing ourselves into a plan for spiritual growth is the wisest decision we can make in life.

My prayer for you is that you will do just that, and that these resources may make a vital contribution to your life.

SO, DON'T SINK YOUR OWN SHIP.
DON'T JUST SIT THERE, DO SOMETHING.

CHAPTER REVIEW

Repetition is the key to mental ownership.

To be free to sail the seven seas, you must make yourself a slave to the compass.

1. Everything you learn t_____ is based on what you learned y_____.
2. Knowledge isn't everything, but everything r_____ on knowledge.
3. Mental r_____ is essential to a t_____ life.
4. We can use neuroscience to g_____ our daily walk with God.

DON'T SINK YOUR OWN SHIP

If something is important, you must repeat it until it changes you.

Chapter Summaries

1. Look to God for h_____.
2. R_____ q_____ when you sin.
3. Be totally o_____ to God.
4. Be a good s_____ of life's resources.
5. Be a s_____ to others.
6. Choose the f_____ of self-discipline.
7. Don't let m_____ become m_____.
8. G_____ your mind to g_____ your life.
9. Use your tongue to h_____, not to h_____.
10. Trust God's definition of s_____.
11. Keep your c_____ clear.
12. Nurture your r_____.
13. Pay the p_____ to be patient.
14. Accept that without p_____ there is no g_____.

15. R_____ your mind to t_____ your life.
16. Don't play c_____ while God is playing c_____.
17. Trust f_____ to guide your life.
18. Trust God and o_____ Him.
19. Don't l_____ with your emotions.
20. Don't just s__ there, d__ something.

 LIFE-CHECK

Answer these questions, either individually by journaling the answer or in a spiritual accountability group.

1. Do you believe you have an adequate foundation of knowledge?
2. Do you believe what you know, and are you living what you believe? What is the greatest strength for you in this area? What is the greatest weakness for you in this area?
3. Do you have a mental renewal system to review truth sufficiently to transform your life? Do you repeat vital truth until it changes you?
4. What is the most important thing you can do for yourself from the list of suggestions from neuroscience?

 FOR FURTHER REFLECTION

Additional Scripture.

Joshua 1:8   Romans 12:2
Psalm 1   2 Timothy 3:16–17
John 8:32   James 1:22

 **RESOURCES**

For further study.

   30 Days to Understanding the Bible, Max Anders

30 Days to Growing in Your Faith, Max Anders
Brave New Discipleship, Max Anders
The Change Zone (www.thechangezone.com)
Switch On Your Brain, Caroline Leaf

HOW TO TEACH THIS BOOK

This book is useful for truth seekers, for new Christians, and for Christians who want to do a "life-check." In fact, it could be used for a periodic life-check, perhaps each January or on vacation, to help you stay on the right path in life. It is written so that it can be used for small group or discipleship study, as well as for individual study.

If you would like to use this book to teach others, you might find the following guidelines helpful. As you read the guidelines, remember that flexibility is the key to their effective use. You may be leading a high-commitment study or a moderate-commitment study. Use the following suggestions as you think best suits your purpose:

1. Begin your time with prayer.
2. Consider having the participant(s) quote from memory the Scripture passage from the first page of the chapter each week. Or this could also be cumulative. That is, the first week the participants quote the Scripture passage from the first chapter; the second week they quote the central passages from the first two chapters, and so on.

   In small discipleship groups or one-on-one sessions, a higher degree of commitment might be required. In larger groups like a Sunday school class where participation is voluntary, less commitment might be required. Adjust your expectations to the group.

3. At the beginning of the session, summarize the chapter in your own words. You might want to bring in information that was not covered in the book.

4. Discuss the material at the end of the chapters as time permits. Use the information that best fits the group.

5. Have a special time for questions and answers, or just encourage questions during the course of discussion. If you are asked a question to which you don't know the answer (it happens to all of us), just say that you don't know but you'll find out. Then on the following week, you can open the question-and-answer time or the discussion time with the answer to the question from the previous week.

6. Close with prayer.

You may have other things you would like to incorporate. Please feel free to do so. Remember: Flexibility is the key to success. These suggestions are intended as a guide, not as a straitjacket.

NOTES

Chapter 1: Look to God for Happiness

1. Blaise Pascal, *Pensees*, trans. W. F. Trotter (Seattle: Pacific Publishing Studio, 2011), 51.
2. Charles Kuralt, *A Life on the Road* (New York: G. P. Putnam's Sons, 1990), 197.
3. Peggy Noonan, *Life, Liberty and the Pursuit of Happiness* (Holbrook, MA: Adams Media Corporation, 1994), 214–15.

Chapter 2: Repent Quickly When You Sin

1. J. I. Packer, *Rediscovering Holiness: Know the Fullness of Life with God* (Ann Arbor, MI: Servant Publications, 1992), 123.
2. Packer, *Rediscovering Holiness*, 121.
3. Packer, *Rediscovering Holiness*, 120.
4. Packer, *Rediscovering Holiness*, 122.
5. Packer, *Rediscovering Holiness*, 136.

Chapter 6: Choose the Freedom of Self-Discipline

1. Peter Hollins, *The Science of Self-Discipline: The Willpower, Mental Toughness, and Self-Control to Resist Temptation and Achieve Your Goals*, self-published, CreateSpace, 2017 (summary).

Chapter 8: Guard Your Mind to Guide Your Life

1. Kitty Harmon, *Up to No Good: The Rascally Things Boys Do* (San Francisco: Chronicle, 2000), 41.

Chapter 10: Trust God's Definition of Success

1. Gary Paulsen, *Winterdance: The Fine Madness of Running the Iditarod* (Orlando, FL: Harcourt, Brace & Co., 1994), 77–78.

Chapter 11: Keep Your Conscience Clear

1. Bob McAlister, "Countdown to Paradise," *Jubilee*, July 1990, 1-3. Used with permission of Prison Fellowship, P.O. Box 17500, Washington, DC 22041–0500.
2. Corrie ten Boom with Jamie Buckingham, *Tramp for the Lord* (Fort Washington, PA: CLC Publications, 1974), 56–57.

Chapter 12: Nurture Your Relationships

1. Ronald Reagan, *An American Life* (New York: Pocket Books, 1990), 262.
2. Harold Kushner, *When All You Ever Wanted Isn't Enough: The Search for a Life That Matters* (New York: Pocket Books, 1986), 165–66.

Chapter 13: Pay the Price to Be Patient

1. William Barclay, *The Letters of James and Peter*, The Daily Study Bible Series, rev. ed. (Louisville, KY: Westminster John Knox Press, 1976), 42–43.

Chapter 14: Accept That without Pain There Is No Gain

1. *Old Yeller*, directed by Robert Stevenson (1957; Santa Clarita, CA: Disney, 2005), DVD.
2. J. I. Packer, *Rediscovering Holiness: Know the Fullness of Life with God* (Ann Arbor, MI: Servant Publications, 1992), 247.

Chapter 15: Renew Your Mind to Transform Your Life

1. Blaise Pascal, *Pensees*, trans. W. F. Trotter (Seattle: Pacific Publishing Studio, 2011), 51.
2. Barry Gordon, "Can We Control Our Thoughts? Why Do Thoughts Pop into My Head as I'm Trying to Fall Asleep?," *Scientific American*, March 1, 2013, https://www.scientificamerican.com/article/can-we -control-our-thoughts/.

3. Benedict Carey, "Who's Minding the Mind?," *New York Times*, July 31, 2007, https://www.nytimes.com/2007/07/31/health /psychology/31subl.html.

4. Caroline Leaf, *Switch On Your Brain: The Key to Peak Happiness, Thinking, and Health* (Grand Rapids: Baker, 2013), 124.

5. Leaf, *Switch On Your Brain*, 128.

Chapter 17: Trust Facts to Guide Your Life

1. Allan Bloom, *The Closing of the American Mind* (New York: Simon and Schuster, 1987).

2. Oprah Winfrey, Golden Globe Lifetime Achievement Award acceptance speech, January 7, 2018.

Chapter 18: Trust God and Obey Him

1. James Herriot, *All Creatures Great and Small* (New York: St. Martin's Press, 1972), 314–15.

Walk Closer with God—Live Better in Life

Let me share a potential vision for your spiritual future.

All motivated Christians would like to be **further down the road**, spiritually, than we currently are. This is how God has made us, after all. But, often, we're not sure what we need to do to advance along this road. Consequently, many believers are hungry for more help in pursuing a richer, fuller walk with the Lord.

In the past, Christians have generally assumed that they could use life's random opportunities to **figure out an overall game plan on their own** for growing to spiritual maturity. But life is much too complicated for that.

Rather, we need a carefully thought-out **strategy** and a **storehouse** of resources to guide and accelerate our spiritual growth.

Thankfully, I have spent most of my life wrestling with this issue and have created resources that will help.

- First, we all have gaps in our **knowledge base**. The Bible says, "the truth will set you free," but this won't happen if you don't know it—or if you don't believe it. I will help you identify and fill in any knowledge gaps you may have and will give you an adequate foundation for advanced spiritual growth (Know).
- Second, we are battling a historic level of cultural brainwashing. Using biblical truth and groundbreaking neurological research, I will give you a **mental renewal system** that will use truth to transform you from the inside out (Be).
- Third, we all need a rich sense of **purpose** in life. I will provide resources to identify your spiritual giftedness and will introduce a process to identify God's call on your life (Do).

The **clearer** our picture is of where we want to go in our Christian life, the more **successful** we will be in getting there.

So, **visit www.maxanders.com** for **strategies** and **resources** to help you *walk closer with God and live better in life.*

Max Anders

30 Days to Understanding the Bible, 30th Anniversary Edition

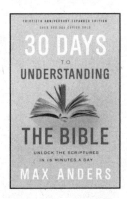

Unlock the Scriptures in 15 Minutes a Day

Max Anders

If you've ever confused the ark of the covenant with the ark of Noah, or Jericho with Jeroboam, Max Anders's classic book *30 Days to Understanding the Bible* is for you. In just fifteen minutes a day, you'll get more out of God's Word by learning the Bible's key people, events, and doctrines. This straightforward and simple-to-use guide has been recommended by Bible teachers and pastors for thirty years, and now it's available in an expanded thirtieth anniversary edition—with the most requested topics from the original edition restored and updated for today's readers.

Features include:

- the "Arc of Bible History," which helps you visualize the Bible's overarching themes
- the "Story of the Bible," which summarizes Genesis through Revelation in just a few pages
- the core beliefs of the Christian faith, focusing on the teachings that have united Christians for the last 2,000 years
- a 13-week plan that provides teachers every creative and effective tool for teaching the Bible in 30 days
- fan-favorite bonus content, which was previously removed but has now been restored from the original edition

Available in stores and online!

30 Days to Growing in Your Faith

Enrich Your Life in 15 Minutes a Day

Max Anders

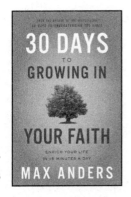

Deepen your faith, strengthen your relationship with God, and enrich your life with this practical guide for spiritual growth.

In *30 Days to Growing in Your Faith*, Max Anders uses a repetition and response methodology to outline a helpful framework for Christian living. To make a complex topic easier to grasp, this book is divided into three sections that reflect the basics of spiritual growth:

- **KNOW:** feed your mind with the truth
- **BE:** integrate your life with the lives of other solid Christians
- **DO:** get up each day and try your best to do what is true and right

Within each of these sections, Max outlines the most important things you need to know, using simple explanations and workbook-style learning to drive biblical truth into the hearts and minds of those who seek it. Here are a few key themes this book addresses:

- eternal perspective and purpose
- desired attitudes, values, and behavior
- responsibilities as followers of Christ

Insightful, engaging, and easy to use, *30 Days to Growing in Your Faith* balances classic Christian teaching with innovative applications for today, giving you a solid foundation for a lifetime of growing in your faith. If you've been wondering how to engage with God's Word in your daily life, this is a must-read.

Available in stores and online!